MW01286354

Improving Your Prayer Life through a Study of the Psalter

Improving Your Prayer Life through a Study of the Psalter

Randall C. Bailey

Foreword by Mark E. Dawson

RESOURCE *Publications* · Eugene, Oregon

IMPROVING YOUR PRAYER LIFE THROUGH A STUDY OF THE PSALTER

Copyright © 2021 Randall C. Bailey. All rights reserved. Except for brief quotations in critical publications or reviews, no part of this book may be reproduced in any manner without prior written permission from the publisher. Write: Permissions, Wipf and Stock Publishers, 199 W. 8th Ave., Suite 3, Eugene, OR 97401.

Resource Publications
An Imprint of Wipf and Stock Publishers
199 W. 8th Ave., Suite 3
Eugene, OR 97401

www.wipfandstock.com

PAPERBACK ISBN: 978-1-6667-1562-0
HARDCOVER ISBN: 978-1-6667-1563-7
EBOOK ISBN: 978-1-6667-1564-4

09/24/21

Scripture quotations are from New Revised Standard Version Bible, copyright © 1989 National Council of the Churches of Christ in the United States of America. Used by permission. All rights reserved worldwide.

Dedicated to my wife, Peggy, in gratitude for over fifty years of a blessed marriage in which she has given support, encouragement, and fortitude to our Christian walk together.

Do not worry about anything, but in everything by prayer and supplication with thanksgiving let your requests be made known to God. And the peace of God, which surpasses all understanding, will guard your hearts and your minds in Christ Jesus.

(PHIL 4:6–7 NRSV)

Let us therefore approach the throne of grace with boldness, so that we may receive mercy and find grace to help in time of need.

(HEB 4:16 NRSV)

Contents

Foreword

WHAT IS A FOREWORD? It is the part you can skip, right? Indeed, you can. Yet, for the author, the publisher, and the potential reader, it is an invitation to read the book, a brief justification of the book. Sometimes the author of a foreword is a person of renown (a famous coach, a doctor, or in this case, one might expect a theologian).

Dr. Bailey certainly is worthy of having a foreword written by a theologian, or an author of many books on religion. On the matter of such credentials, Dr. Randall "Randy" Bailey needs no confirmation from me, as you can see from his scholarly achievements and life of service and leadership as noted in the biographical note.

The invitation to write the foreword is a testimony to Randy's motivation for writing the book in the first place—not for fame or accolades from his peers, but rather to be of service to his fellow believers in Christ. What I bring to the table, humbly, is the fact that I recently taught the book in manuscript as part of an adult Sunday school class at the congregation where I worship. I have worked as a teacher of English at the college level, and for many years as an aide to a busy US congressperson. As a layperson, I have led several dozen Sunday school classes. As a part of these experiences, I have had numerous opportunities to witness the reactions, good and bad, to various kinds of texts.

Regarding this book, I am convinced of its unique nature, and its efficacy both for the individual, for small groups, for adult Sunday school classes, and for church leaders. I am pleased to say that in my class experience, every participant found the book to be deeply thoughtful, and both provocative and challenging in the best sense of those words.

As with a great movie, I want to share things about the book without giving away the delightful surprises, and without imposing my conclusions on parts of the book which are meant for meditation by each individual reader.

First, while there are books about Psalms, and books about prayer, I am not aware of another book like this. Randy asks us to read the psalms, and read New Testament admonitions (and encouragements) to be bold in our prayer life, and then to ask ourselves this question: "Am I being as bold as the speakers/authors of the psalms?" If not, I am opting not to avail myself of the benefits God wants me to have from my prayer life. Introductory sections enable the reader to understand the types of psalms, and the fundamental structure used by the writers (for example, using parallel lines of poetry to express a similar thought twice, though with a variation or affirmation in the second line). Similarly, there are terms to ponder, such as *piety*. In other words, what is my view of God when I open that "door" of prayer and speak to him? What do I expect to happen? What did the psalmists expect to happen? Am I expecting less of God than did the authors of the psalms? If so, I am missing the richness of prayer.

Second, while the Psalter includes prayers of obvious, individual pleading and meditation, there are psalms meant for public, group consumption. Thus, the book allows readers to ponder how an individual's view of God, his or her piety, differs from or harmonizes with that of the local body of Christ where they worship. This recalls Proverbs 27:17, "one man sharpens another" (ESV). The richer my prayer life, the better equipped I am to encourage my spiritual brothers and sisters. Likewise, the better equipped a minister, deacon, elder, or other ministry leader is to lead and to manage.

The reader will find that the book is also a call to courage, not unlike Moses encouraging Joshua. There are many opportunities for each reader to meditate on New Testament verses that harmonize with studying the Psalms. While the Psalms are inspired, they are not often written with the apparent purpose of outlining theological arguments. They are the records of the outpouring of the human heart seeking God—and strong reminders that there is no one else, certainly no other "god," to whom we should turn. Do I have the courage to examine myself and to speak plainly, even when troubled, to my Creator, who also is my Savior? As Peter says in John 6:68, when Jesus asks the Twelve if they also want to leave him (as crowds of disciples had just done), "Lord, to whom shall we go?" (ESV)

Finally, from a utilitarian standpoint, Randy provides well-ordered material followed by questions at the end of each chapter. Thus, I find another aspect of the book's unique appeal to be the fact that it is useful for individual study and meditation, as well as for provocative and faith-building group discussions.

As a fellow Christian worker alongside Randy (with Randy as the planner and leader) in Ukraine some years ago, I have seen and experienced Randy's humble love for God and his godly desire to be of service to his brothers and sisters. You will find your reading of this book to be time well spent in pursuit of those same goals.

Mark E. Dawson
Washington, DC
2021

Acknowledgments

I OWE MANY THANKS to Dr. Paul Riemann (deceased 2019), whose Psalms Seminar in 1983 introduced me to these issues, to the many professors and scholars whose mentoring and works have opened my eyes to the possibilities of using the Psalter to improve my prayer live, to the many students who have explored these issues with me in our class discussions, and who have presented this material in their Sunday school classes, to the various churches that encouraged weekend Psalms and Prayer Seminars where this work could be honed, and to my family (children, their spouses, and children) who have always been an encouragement to me to seek to improve my service to God. Indeed, this work is the summation of their influence and places me in debt to all of them.

Introduction

The Dynamics of Prayer

HOW SHALL WE PRAY? What happens when we pray? Do we believe that our prayers may change God's mind? People in every place and time have raised these and similar questions. I went through a similar process several years ago upon completing an intense period of academic study. In reflecting on my prayer life, I often wondered whether my prayers even mattered. Such questioning is not a new phenomenon. Note the disciple's question in Luke 11:1. Jesus "was praying in a certain place, and when he finished, one of his disciples said to him, 'Lord, teach us to pray, as John taught his disciples'" (NRSV).

We have heard this passage since we were children. The example of John the Baptist, who had taught his disciples to pray, created in this disciple a desire for a similar lesson. Evidently, he thought, or knew, he was missing something. I believe many of us, like this disciple, have felt we are missing something. Jesus did not hesitate but gave the instructions known as the "Model Prayer" (vv. 2–4). Matthew 6:9–12 expands the prayer. There Jesus taught the disciples to pray, giving God proper honor, for the kingdom (church), that God's will be done, for forgiveness as we forgive others, and for strength in trying times. We have learned these subjects well. Luke makes clear that Jesus also gave instructions that we have not learned so well. In Luke 11:5–13, he illustrates with the parable of a friend at midnight how we should ask specifically, directly, and boldly for things that are of concern to us. We should argue for things we think we need, as corroborated in Hebrews 4:15–16. We should take comfort that, unlike the friend at midnight, who only responded due to the friend's persistence, God is ready to engage in dialogue with us and give us everything we need. Similarly, we should take comfort in the fact that just as we "who are evil, know how to give good gifts to [our] children, how much more will the heavenly Father give the Holy Spirit to those who ask him!" (Luke 11:13 NRSV). In studying these passages, we have learned to pray persistently, but failed to understand the qualities inherent in that boldness. In short, we have learned well *what to pray*, but less well *how to pray*.

The Purpose of the Study

This study explores the dynamics of our prayer life and compares that to the "prayer psalms"[1] to see whether we pray in a manner like the psalmists or more in line with our preconceived ideas of God's sovereignty, particularly his foreknowledge. Hopefully, the investigation of these issues will result in an improved prayer life for the reader.

Particularly, we explore such ideas as *social reality* (the social and theological dynamics when we are in the act of praying or worship), *piety* (the view we have of God when we pray or worship), and the *I/Thou* relationship (the bond between individuals and God that serves as the foundation for prayer). We will explore the so-called *individual* and *communal lament* (often called "complaint") psalms. Individuals and communities pray these prayers during times of crisis. Their goal is to influence God to fix the situation in which they find themselves. *Individual/communal praise* psalms arise from individuals and communities in response to God having answered previous prayers, or because God is God. The identification marker for deciding whether a psalm is an

---

1. Riemann, *Dissonant Pieties*, 1. This is the term coined by Riemann and defined in note 1. The term is especially applicable to this study. Riemann preferred the term "plaint psalms" instead of the more common "complaint psalms." This study employs both terms with the same meaning.

individual psalm is whether the singular or plural pronoun is used (e.g., "I" vs. "we").

Epigraphs

I employ two epigraphs—Philippians 4:6–7 and Hebrews 4:15–16.

> Do not worry about anything, but in everything by prayer and supplication with thanksgiving let your requests be made known to God. And the peace of God, which surpasses all understanding, will guard your hearts and your minds in Christ Jesus. (Phil 4:6–7 NRSV)

> For we do not have a high priest who is unable to sympathize with our weaknesses, but we have one who in every respect has been tested as we are, yet without sin. Let us therefore approach the throne of grace with boldness, so that we may receive mercy and find grace to help in time of need. (Heb 4:15–16 NRSV)

Paul defines precisely what we might call "a prayer cycle" in Philippians 4:6–7. Here he details the different aspects of prayer. *What we should pray,* "supplication with thanksgiving . . . [and] requests." Practiced correctly, these produce the "peace of God," and involve every detail of our lives, whether specific requests when trouble arises, or thanks for answered prayer.

The Hebrews writer further indicates that our prayer life should be one of "boldness" (NRSV) or "confidence" (ESV and many translations) because Jesus can "sympathize with our weaknesses" for "in every respect" he has "been tested as we are, yet without sin." This sympathy (empathy?) serves as the foundation for the admonishment in v. 16, "approach the throne of grace with boldness" when we have the need. So, the *how we should pray* must involve "boldness/confidence." The Hebrews writer had been discussing how the disobedience of Israel kept many people from entering the promised land (vv. 1–10). In v. 11, he exhorted the Hebrew Christians not to make the same mistake: "Let use therefore strive to enter that rest, so that no one may fall by the same sort of disobedience." He continues to explain that the word of God makes all our hidden actions and thoughts known and open (vv. 12–13). Then he concludes in vv. 14–16 that Jesus' sacrifice on our behalf should produce boldness in our prayer lives. When compared to the psalmists' attitude in prayer this command to be bold in prayer, may cause us difficulty in understanding what "boldness" means. Stated frankly, sometimes I think we pray timidly because we have not studied how the psalmists prayed. When we do, we find that the psalmists' prayers seem to be bold, outrageous, impertinent, and at times disrespectful. (Actually this may be evidence of a close relationship with God.) Yet the psalmists did not have the advantage we do. In their day, Jesus had not yet come and demonstrated his empathy for our struggles through his life, death, and resurrection. In our day, we have the assurance from the Hebrews writer of Jesus' empathy which should make us bolder in our prayer lives than the psalmists.

We do *what to pray* well, but do not do *how to pray* nearly as well. We pray, with supplications, thanksgivings, making requests to God that he will guard, guide, and direct us. Exactly what does "guard, guide, and direct us" mean? Further, the norm seems to be that we pray mostly for others rather than ourselves. When we do pray for ourselves we find it difficult to be specific in our prayers. That is, we find it difficult "boldly" to make "supplications" that contain precise "requests" asking God to fix the problem in a particular way. The epigraphs serve to focus us on this goal of improving our prayer lives.

To illustrate the power of these two epigraphs, note the following:

1. Lament/complaint/plaint/prayer psalms comprise nearly half of the psalms

2. We find little to none of these in our hymnals; at least I do not know of any, do you?

3. These two facts indicate the psalmists may have understood something we do not.

4. The different psalmists' prayers seem to exhibit a boldness that is superior to our prayers, even though the Hebrews writer implied we should be bolder than they.

5. Since the Hebrews writer said we should approach God boldly because Jesus' sacrifice produced his empathy for us, the implication is we should not be timid (like the psalmists?), but bold in our approach to God in prayer.

Readers should meditate on and process these verses. As they proceed through each lesson they should seek to apply their new understanding to improve their prayer lives.

Academics Made Practical

I have taught earlier versions of the following lessons in Sunday school classes several times, as well as offering weekend Psalm and Prayer Seminars for several churches. All the experiences seemed successful, since the participants happily observed because the material is a little more challenging it led them deeper into studies of prayer than traditional Sunday school classes. Positive comments by former students and friends who also have taught earlier versions of this material seem to corroborate this conclusion. This success seems to point to individuals in churches who want to study a little deeper than usually occurs in such classes and therefore provides added opportunities for these individuals to improve their prayer lives.

In recent years biblical and theological academicians have produced many studies that contain great practical value. I have sought to make some of this research available to the critical-thinking layperson. Hopefully, creating this opportunity for Christians who seek to improve their prayer lives will lead to an improvement in both public and private prayers and worship.

Among these, two scholars hold a preeminence for me due to the watershed moments they created for me in my journey to improve my understanding and practice of prayer. My prayer struggle began after the successful completion of a ThM thesis on predestination, the foreknowledge of God, and humanity's free will. Upon completion of this project, I began to question whether my prayers could change God's mind. Specifically stated, my struggle was, "After all, if God knows everything, how can my prayers change God's mind?" The first watershed moment occurred in a PhD seminar on the Psalter with Dr. Paul Riemann. In one of his first lectures he compared Psalm 30 to Calvin's statements regarding prayer.[2] Here I found some of the answers which I sought. During the next several years, I struggled to come to a better understanding of these relationships. The next watershed moment was in reading Samuel E. Balentine's *Prayer in the Hebrew Bible*. Balentine's observations are especially useful since he focuses "primarily on prose and nonpsalmic prayers."[3] This creates a fertile ground for the application for a nonacademic audience of his observations and conclusions in a study of the prayer psalms of the Psalter. Hopefully, this study and its use of these sources will aid all readers to pray more boldly, earnestly, openly, and reverently, looking for God's answers to their prayers.

Lessons

Lesson 1 introduces the Psalter. Lesson 2 explores the "Dynamics of Prayer Life," addressing the question, "What happens when we pray?" Specifically, it examines how different individuals think, observe, and practice prayer. Lesson 3 introduces the concepts of *social reality, piety* and the *I/Thou* relationships, summarizing and comparing the Psalter's views of these concepts with Calvin's and many modern Christians'; it seeks to see how these concepts affect the prayer life of the Christian. Lesson 4 applies this material by showing that a better understanding of God presupposes an improvement in our social reality, piety, and prayer life. Lesson 5 introduces individual lament, exploring what happens when

2. This lecture Riemann later published in a Festschrift for Dr. Herbert B. Huffmon as "Dissonant Pieties," 354–400, eventually published in the monograph *Dissonant Pieties*, xi–82. Citations are from the monograph.

3. Balentine, *Prayer*, 13.

the individual hurts; it investigates how several individual lament psalms may serve as a model for suffering individuals as they pray to God regarding their suffering. Lesson 6 introduces communal lament, examining what happens when the community hurts; it explores how communal lament may serve as a model for the suffering community as it prays to God regarding its suffering. Lesson 7 takes up the theme of the Psalter's prayers versus Calvin's view of prayer, and their influence on modern Christians, seeking to understand how a more refined social reality and piety creates a better foundation for the proper practice of lament by modern Christians. Lesson 8 examines individual praise, raising such questions as "Why do we praise God?" and "Does God need our praise?" It examines Psalm 30 as an example of individual praise. Lesson 9 considers psalms that provide examples of proper communal praise and their significance in such contexts as corporate worship. Lesson 10 synthesizes the preceding material describing the inherent characteristics of social reality, piety lament, praise, and their impact on our piety in private prayer and public worship. Lesson 11 offers a summary and conclusions, seeking to demonstrate how this study may improve our prayer and worship.

Questions for Further Study

The purpose of categories of questions (opening, reflection, visualization, and action) is to provoke thought and discussion as students dig deeper into their prayer lives. Placed at the end of each lesson, including this introduction (should a teacher desire to use it as one of the class sessions) they invite students to engage in self-assessment of their ideas of private and personal prayers in private and public worship. The *opening* questions invite students to assess their thoughts on the subject at hand. The *reflection* questions invite students to compare and contrast their assessment with the discussion in the classroom. The *visualization* questions prompt students to consider how their prayers and relationships might change with God if they revise their perspective on the subject discussed. The *action* questions encourage students to put into practice the new things learned. This means the students and teachers should take opportunity to repeat, rewrite, or add to these questions as needed. Similarly, though there are twelve lessons (counting this introduction) some lessons are longer and more challenging, making this study capable of continuing beyond one quarter of study

Questions for Further Study: With the epigraphs in mind consider the following questions:

Opening

1. What is your attitude regarding prayer? Do you believe your prayers can change God's mind? Do you believe you should make such requests? How do you think your views of prayer relate to the prayer-psalms?

2. What does Jesus' model prayer in Luke 11:1–13 teach us about prayer?

Reflection

1. How do you believe social reality impacts worship and prayer? Have you ever considered that in every church worship and group Bible study, public and private prayers have their own social reality or personality? How do you think these influence worship practices?

2. How do you believe your piety (your view of God), affects your worship? When someone says, "God," what image comes to mind? How do you believe your view of God influences your prayers and worship?

3. Do you see how your piety affects how you pray, especially how you address God, as well as dictating the things you will or will not ask of him?

Visualization

1. Have you ever considered your I/Thou? That is, when you pray and worship have you ever considered how you viewed your relationship with God, how you saw yourself before God, and how this understanding affected your worship and prayer life?

2. Do you understand you must imagine together the social reality, piety, and I/Thou? That is, do you understand that they must be congruent if you are going to be pleased with your worship practices and prayer life?

3. Do you understand how comparing our worship and prayer life attitudes to those of the prayer-psalms will help us improve our prayer lives and worship? Can you perceive some areas where this may occur?

4. How do you understand the epigraphs? How can we be bolder in our prayer lives? Do we boldly pray for God to change our situations and then thank him when he does?

Action

1. Can you anticipate any ways your prayer life and worship will improve as you proceed through this study?

2. Create a list of lessons learned from this introductory lesson. As we continue through this study, add to and modify this list to track improvements in your prayer life.

1

Introduction to the Psalter

The Names of the Psalter

THE WORDS "PSALMS" AND "psalter" are anglicized forms of the Latin *psalmi* and *psalterium*, which themselves derive from the Greek *psalmoi* and *psalterion*. *Psalterion*, originally referred to a stringed instrument, but later came to mean a "collection of songs." These terms apparently translated the Hebrew term *mizmôr*, which indicated a religious song accompanied by stringed instrument(s). In the Hebrew Bible, the book's title is *sepher těhillîm* (book of praises).[1] The Psalter was by no means unique in the ancient Near East or in the religious realm today. The various cultures of the ancient Near East possessed a similar body of literature. Christendom in general has similar material, expressed in their hymnals. The Psalter was Israel's hymnal. This fact has great implications for us in terms of our prayer life and worship. Because the Psalter is a hymnal, we should always cite the individual psalms by their numbers, "Psalm 1," "Psalm 2," and the like. We should not cite individual psalms as "chapters."

---

1. Mowinckel, *Psalms*, 2:207–10.

Place of the Psalms in the Old Testament

The Hebrew Bible divides into three parts: law, prophets, and writings. Note Luke's record of Jesus' words in Luke 24:44, "Then he said to them, 'These are my words that I spoke to you while I was still with you—that everything written about me in the law of Moses, the prophets, and the psalms must be fulfilled'" (NRSV). The Hebrew Bible divides into three main sections: law, prophets, and writings. The Psalms occur first in the Writings. English Bibles do not follow this organization. Rather the Psalms come right after the book of Job, which itself follows the books of history (Joshua–Esther).

Organization and Interesting Facts about the Psalms

Though we often refer to the "Psalms of David," as if he wrote all of them, several different authors wrote the psalms. Several psalms appear to be nearly identical. These include: (1) 14 and 53; (2) 40:13–17 and 70:1–5; (3) 108 and 57:7–11. Psalm 72:20 states, "The prayers of David, the son of Jesse, are ended" (NRSV) yet there are other psalms with "of David" in the title, such as 108–10.

Some psalms favor the name "YHWH," while other parts favor the term "God." Book 1 uses YHWH (Yahweh, Jehovah) over *Elohim* (God) in a ratio of 272 to 15. Book 2 uses *Elohim* over YHWH in a ratio of 162 to 30. According to Leupold, "the use of the divine names as well as other factors indicate that at the time" of the subscription of 72:20, "two distinct books were already in existence, and presumably of the same scope and compass that they now have."[2]

The Psalter is a collection of five different books: book 1 = 1–41; book 2 = 42–72; book 3 = 73–89; book 4 = 90–106; book 5 = 107–50. These five books evolved within three broad periods.[3] (1) Preexilic psalms show affinities with the Ugaritic poetic material.[4]

2. Leupold, *Psalms*, 3.

3 Harrison, *Introduction*, 984–85.

4. Ras Shamra, Ugarit, is an archaeological site in modern-day Syria. In

These psalms deal with the king and kingship; some scholars label these "royal psalms," while other scholars designate these "messianic psalms," and apply them to Jesus. (2) Psalms whose contents reveal a time in the exile are exilic. (3) Psalms whose contents reveal a period after the exile are postexilic. Evidently, the ongoing enlargement of the Psalter continued during these three periods until it took its present form. Interestingly, each of these books closes with a doxology (praise), while Psalm 150 constitutes "an appropriate doxology to the Psalter as a whole."[5] If we regard Psalm 1 as the introduction to the Psalter then the entire book reveals a structure that moves from an introduction (Ps 1) through the various psalms of lament and praise, to praise (Ps 150). Some have suggested that this fivefold division is an imitation of the five books of the Law of Moses.[6] This final compilation probably occurred about the third century BCE. Interestingly, the Septuagint and the Hebrew text both have 150 psalms, but their enumeration differs.

Hebrew	LXX
1–8	1–8
9–10	9
11–113	10–112
114–15	113
116:1–9	114

the 1920s a new language was discovered there, now called "Ugaritic." This language is as close to biblical Hebrew as modern French and Spanish are to Latin. Further, the language gives us great insight into the worship of Ba'al, the god of the Sidonians, which Jezebel imported into Israel during the prophet Elijah's days, as 1 Kgs 16:31 observes: "[Ahab] took for his wife Jezebel the daughter of Ethbaal king of the Sidonians, and went and served Baal and worshiped him" (NRSV).

5. Harrison, *Introduction*, 986.

6. Anderson, *Psalms*, 1:27.

Hebrew	LXX
116:10–19	115
117–46	116–45
147:1–11	146
147:12–20	147
148–50	150
	(151)

The LXX's adds an extra psalm, numbered 151, described as "outside the number."[7] This may indicate the closing of the Psalter, pointing to its canonical status.

Hebrew Poetry

The student of the Psalter must be familiar with the basic elements of Hebrew poetry. Hebrew poetry's predominant structure is parallelism, in which the second line repeats or refers to the first in some way. The relationship between the lines serves to provide insight into the meaning of the text. This is the Hebrew way of thinking; parallelism also occurs in Hebrew narrative. Here Gen 1:27 (NRSV), with italics and bold text, highlights this relationship.

> Line 1: *So God created humankind [Heb. Adam]* **in his image**,
> Line 2: **in the image of God** *he created them* [Heb. *him*];
> Line 3: **male and female** *he created them*.

The NRSV, due to its gender-neutral language, translates the Hebrew "Adam" (*'adām*) as "humankind," and the Hebrew pronoun "him" is changed to "them." Though acceptable, this does not capture the full power of the Hebrew parallelism. Movement

---

7. Anderson, *Psalms*, 1:27.

occurs among the three lines. The traditional translation, "Adam," is more cogent than the NRSV's, "humankind." "Adam" interacts with the Hebrew poetry, allowing the various parallel lines to serve as commentary on one another. Such parallelism is not just a re-statement of previous lines; rather it further defines those lines. Lines 1 and 2 emphasize that only God created man—"God cre-ated Adam" and "he created him" (that is the male). Lines 1 and 2 further emphasize that the creation of this male was in God's image—"in his image" and "in the image of God." Lines 1 and 3 emphasize that God's creation "in his image" involves the creation of the male and female sexes (humankind)—"in his image" and "male and female." Lines 2 and 3 reinforce this thought with the phrases "image of God" paralleling "male and female," while "he created him" parallels "he created them." Specifically, parallelism allows the differing lines to serve as commentaries on the others.

This illustration demonstrates just how complex parallelism can be. The student who reads biblical poetry gains greater insight by stopping and comparing the parallelisms to see how they high-light the text. This is especially true of the Psalter's poetry. Students who take the time to investigate parallelism in the Psalter receive a greater benefit from their study. Additionally, understanding He-brew poetry gives further insight into the power of Jesus' parables. In the parables, he gives line 1 by telling the parable. The audience was to supply line 2 as their conclusion. As an example, Jesus said in Matt 13:44, "The kingdom of heaven is like treasure hidden in a field, which a man found and hid; then in his joy he goes and sells all that he has and buys that field" (NRSV). The audience should supply the second line or parallelism by answering the unstated question, "What is the value of the kingdom, is it worth all you possess?"

Finally, one of the definitions of Hebrew poetry is it "is an artificial language" that "does not follow the normal rules of communication."[8] As such, "poetry is a form of discourse that expresses powerful or profound emotions and feelings."[9] Since poetry does not communicate facts as much as it does emotions,

8. Longman and Dillard, *Introduction*, 26.
9. Petersen and Richards, *Hebrew Poetry*, 8.

its figurative, symbolic, opened-ended language allows multiple interpretations, in which the reader may identify with the emotions expressed in a manner not acceptable in the other parts of the Bible.

One of the most obvious examples occurs in Ps 51:5, "Indeed, I was born guilty, a sinner when my mother conceived me" (NRSV). Undeniably, this translation and many other versions correctly and literally translate this passage. Therefore, many argue this literal translation teaches that infants inherit the sin of Adam. Yet, we must remember this poetic statement expresses the feelings of the author, which the title attributes to David when Nathan confronted him regarding his sin. Since this is poetry, the passage is stating how the author felt, not the doctrine of hereditary total depravity. He felt as if he "was born guilty" (NIV, "sinful at birth"), and beyond that, "a sinner when my mother conceived me" (NRSV). That is how he felt, but he was wrong! To translate the passage literally is to render the English translation as closely as possible to the Hebrew. To interpret the passage's meaning correctly we must take its poetry into account. So, for the passage to prove the doctrine of hereditary total depravity it must be descriptive, not of the author, but of all humankind. In short, the Hebrew and the English translation must state something like, "All humankind is sinful at birth, sinful from the time their mothers conceived them." Yet the passage does not say that. So, it cannot refer to humankind. To illustrate this inconsistency, if anyone who cites Ps 51:5 as evidence that humankind is born in sin, that individual must also argue that the statement in Ps 22:6, "I am a worm," must mean that the psalmist (and all humankind for that matter) was and is a real worm! To do otherwise is to engage in an inconsistent hermeneutic in which we argue that Ps 51:5, though poetic, is literal in meaning, thus teaching the doctrine of hereditary total depravity, while Ps 22:6, because it employs symbolic language and metaphor, is poetic and figurative. We must recognize that the Psalter makes extensive use of metaphor, simile, and the like to describe the various psalmists' feelings, which may not have been true. Their expressed emotional views might be in direct violation of biblical principles.

Psalm Titles and Terms

Some psalms have titles, while others do not. Those that have a name (possible author?) associated with them may be listed as follows: (1) Asaph (73–83); (2) David (3–41, 51–65, 68–70, 86, 100, 103, 108–10, 122, 124, 138–45); (3) Ethan (89); (4) Korahites (45–49, 84–85, 87–88); (5) Moses (90); (6) Solomon (72, 127). Those that have no name associated with them are 1–2, 42–44, 66–67, 71, 91–90, 102, 104–7, 111–21, 123, 125–26, 128–30, 132–37, and 146–50.

To argue that "of David" means David wrote a specific psalm can create problems. In Psalm 34, the title indicates the king before whom David simulated madness was Abimlech, whereas 1 Sam 21:10 names the king as Achish. Similarly, the title of Psalm 56 seems to imply that the Philistine captured David and brought him to Gath, whereas in 1 Sam 21:10, David fled there of his own initiative.[10]

Some psalm titles have descriptions that attempt to classify them in a manner like what occurs in the back of our hymnals. "Psalm" (*mizmôr*) occurs fifty-seven times and is a technical term, perhaps a song sung to the accompaniment of instruments. "Shiggaion" (*šiggāyôn*) occurs only in Psalm 7 and may be a lamentation. "Miktam" (*miktām*) occurs in Psalms 16 and 56–60 and is perhaps a psalm of atonement. "Prayer" (*tepillâ*) occurs in Psalms 17, 86, 90, 102, and 142, and is perhaps a lamentation. "Song" (*šîr*) occurs in 69:30 and is a common term for both religious and secular songs. "Maskil" (*maśkîl*) occurs in Psalms 32, 42, 44, 45, 52, 53, 54, 55, 74, 78, 88, 89, and 142, and may be a didactic psalm. "Song of praise" (*šîr mizmôr*) occurs only in Psalm 145. "A love song" (*šîr yědîdot*) occurs in Psalm 45. "A Song of Ascents" (*šîr hamma'ălôt*) occurs in Psalms 120–34 and may refer to songs sung on the way to worship.

Paul exhorts to "sing psalms and hymns and spiritual songs among ourselves, singing and making melody to the Lord with your hearts" (Eph 5:19 NRSV). When Paul mentions "psalms and

---

10. Harrison, *Introduction*, 977.

hymns and spiritual songs" he is giving a general classification that encompasses the smaller breakdown of the nine descriptions above.

"Selāh" occurs seventy times (e.g., 3, 4, 7, 9, 20, 21, 24, 32, 39, 44, 46–50, 52, 54, 55, 57, 59–62, 66–68, 75–77, 81–85, 87–89, 140, 143) and serves as a musical term of some kind that still puzzles scholars. We should not read it when we read the psalms publicly. To read it publicly would be equivalent to singing the notes in our hymnals as we sing the song.

The Use of the Psalms in the New Testament[11]

The Psalter is one of the Old Testament books most often quoted by the New Testament. The quotations usually come from the Septuagint. This results in different thought and wording. The New Testament citations usually apply the psalm to Christ, based on a key word (2:7, son; 8:4, son of man; 34:9, Lord). These psalm passages "are often lifted from their original settings and 'reinterpreted' in an entirely different sense" in the New Testament, indicating they "were understood in the early church in completely new ways."[12] Therefore, we should not interpret the Psalms only from the New Testament perspective, reading this meaning back into them. Rather, we should attempt to understand what the psalm meant originally to the Israelites of the day, and then explore how the New Testament applies it to Christian life. These concepts will become more apparent in the following discussion.

Psalm Types

Traditionally, scholars have grouped the various psalms into types or topics for their study. *Communal lament/complaint* psalms arise because of some calamity threatening the well-being of the community, motivating it to pray prayers that would pressure God to correct the situation. *Individual lament/complaint* psalms, "the

11. Ash and Miller, *Psalms*, 28–30.

12. Ash and Miller, *Psalms*, 28.

backbone of the Psalter,"[13] reflect an individual's suffering, producing prayers to God designed to influence him to correct the situation. The individual is in great distress, often ill, and surrounded by enemies, a situation very much like that found in Job, or that of Hannah in 1 Samuel 1. There are two specific features of this class. (1) The *certainty of hearing*, not always present, but points to a change in attitude from despair and complaint to joy and praise. (2) A description of some kind of illness, which makes use of such figurative language that the reader has difficulty determining "the immediate cause of the psalmist's trouble," but the fear of death is of utmost concern.[14] The commonly expressed idea "that, if Yahweh is not directly responsible, he has at least permitted it," which results in the psalmist "either confessing his sin or affirming his innocence," and pleading with God to deliver "the suppliant from his straits or freeing him, as it were, from prison."[15] There are about seventy-five (50 percent of the Psalter) that are lament psalms compared to few to none in our hymnals. In *communal praise* psalms, the community, either due to a specific event or in their general worship, offers praise and thanksgiving to God for answered prayers. *Individual praise* psalms indicate that the individual worshiper, due to some good fortune, offers praise and thanksgiving to God for granting past requests and blessings, as Hannah experienced in 1 Samuel 2. These individual and communal praise and lament psalms, scholars often designate as "prayer psalms."[16]

The designations "individual" and "communal" provide a simple way to classify the psalms based on whether the psalmist employed the singular or plural first-person pronoun. Without doubt, some individuals wrote songs for private use, which later moved into the public use; these employ the singular pronoun "I" and likely occurred in public worship. Other psalms originated for public use from the beginning and employ the pronoun "we." However, this distinction is not as emphatic as it sounds. As

13. Johnson, "Psalms," 169.

14. Johnson, "Psalms," 170–71.

15. Johnson, "Psalms," 171.

16. Riemann, *Dissonant Pieties*, 1.

Watson observes, "Sometimes, the use of the first-person singular may simply be a device adopted by the poet in order to engage his audience."[17] Modern hymns illustrate this point. "Amazing Grace that saved a wretch like *me*," though sung publicly, just does not work as "Amazing Grace that saved wretches like *us*." John Newton wrote the hymn to explain how God could save him, a former slave trader then turned preacher. On the other hand, we do sing, "When *we* all get to heaven," not "When *I* get to heaven." So, while "we" and "I" help classify these psalms, we should also stop sometimes and ask, "To whom do the 'I' or 'we' refer when we sing such songs?"

Hymns functioned in Israel's worship in a way like that found in modern worship. As noted earlier, royal psalms, or messianic psalms, mention the king in some fashion and seem to define the royal aspects of Jesus' ministry. Both types of psalms involve praise of God because *he is God*, and not for any specific act for which the psalmist gives thanks. We will not focus so much on hymns, but will focus on the individual and communal praise and lament psalms in our study.

Uses of the Praise and Lament Prayer Psalms

Praise and lament are expressions of two extremes of the human/divine relationship; they are the dominant categories of the psalms.[18] Some of the laments (3, 4, 5, 7, 17, 26, 27, 54, 55, and 69) may have involved accused individuals who prayed to God against his enemies (accusers) and received from the priests the verdict of God. Can you find the correct verses in the above psalms? Some of the laments (4, 6, 7, 11, 17, 23, 26, 27, 57, and 63) seem to be pleas for divine judgment that ask for protection. Can you find the correct verses in the above psalms?

Several of the psalms do deal with sick people (6, 13, 22, 28, and 102:3–7). These psalms represent prayers for preservation and healing. The authors very seldom confess guilt in their

17. Watson, "Hebrew Poetry," 256.
18. Westermann, *Praise and Lament*, 154.

laments, but they praise God for answering their prayer and restoring their health.

Many of the psalms have characteristics that make them useful in "group therapy."[19] Two factors come into play: (1) the relationship of the individual to the group; (2) the relationship between word and act in religious matters. This approach sees the value in trained professionals whose goal was the rehabilitation of the individual as a member of his/her primary social sphere (clan or family). This approach compares the rehabilitation of the sufferer in the Old Testament to contemporary group-therapy movements. This approach seeks to reintegrate a distressed person into the primary group through a process of words and actions under a group leader. This approach opens new avenues of investigation and application in today's world of the church. In this context, the lament psalms exhibit elements of the death-grief process observed in terminally patients; they are thus very useful for persons handling loss, grief, and death.[20]

Identification Problems

Should we designate these psalms "laments-complaints," or "petitions-supplications"? Thinking of them as laments-complaints portrays these as functioning primarily to lay out complaint against God and others, articulating the human need, and giving form to the anguish and despair of one in trouble. Thinking of them as petitions-supplications categorizes these prayers as placing before God specific petitions for help in the hope and expectation that God will intervene in the situation to deliver one from trouble.[21]

The emphasis given to one over the other may tend to affect one's theology of prayer in one of two ways. (1) It "may tend to create an understanding of prayer as an expression of human distress and

19. Gerstenberger, *Der bittende Mensch*; see also Miller, *Interpreting the Psalms*, 7.

20. Miller, *Interpreting the Psalms*, 7; see also Brueggemann, "Formfulness of Grief," 263–75.

21. Miller, *Interpreting the Psalms*, 9.

a struggle with God that is in itself healing and restorative, and a notion of God as present and involved in suffering more than delivering persons out of it." (2) "Or one's sense of these prayers as petitions for help may focus one's theology on prayer as effective in bringing about the power of God, who is able to deliver and does so."[22] Therefore, an individual's theology of prayer may influence how that person understands the psalms, as well as how he or she prays.

The Fundamental Human Needs Portrayed in the Psalter

How do the psalms identify the fundamental human needs? Only a few of the psalms identify the condition of the lamenter with sin, and many are either ambiguous or list other factors. According to Miller, the issue has been complicated due to the influence of New Testament theology and its "understanding of the person and work of Christ." The focus of New Testament theologians has been on Jesus' work of salvation, not the "ending of human suffering," although the New Testament uses Psalm 22 to understand the suffering of Christ.[23]

Miller goes on to describe the variety of figurative language, because it occurs without a historical context, creates the possibility of an ongoing reinterpretation even to the present. Expressions such as the hidden face of God, his forgetting, being silent, and the like (usually understood in terms of divine judgment of sin as in the prophetic texts) do not seem to possess this meaning in the psalms. Because Christians emphasize Rom 3:23—"all have sinned and come short of the glory of God" (NRSV)—they have about as much trouble with the claims of innocence as they do with imprecations against enemies (cf. Psalm 137). Such issues may subordinate the issue of sin to claims of covenantal relationship to God.[24]

22. Miller, *Interpreting the Psalms*, 9.

23. Miller, *Interpreting the Psalms*, 9–10.

24. Miller, *Interpreting the Psalms*, 10.

The Psalter contains a great variety of themes. Its literature, by its very nature (words spoken to God, or about God), allows greater liberty in interpretation. New Testament writers often reinterpret them very differently from the original form and function. Expressions such as "fearing God," "God as refuge," "the poor," "the afflicted," and the like may have originally described persons who were oppressed and afflicted, while in a later stage came to mean the pious nation, and finally, today can be adapted by the twenty-first-century pious individual who identifies with these concepts and feelings. Such stereotypical language as the various psalms exemplify may open the door for an ongoing process of interpretation! Examples of such reinterpretation occur in the various psalm titles as well as the Christian community's identification with certain feelings and emotions as represented by the "I" psalms.[25]

The Variety of the Psalms

The book has great variety: (1) prayers and petitions addressed to God; (2) praise of God that usually addresses him in the third person; (3) thanksgiving addressed to God; (4) divine speech addressed to the worshipers(s); (5) proclamations to the audience; (6) descriptions of worship.

The Psalter's universality needs more attention because its literature strikes at the basic human emotions that exude such a general familiarity that people feel more comfortable with various psalms than they do with other parts of the Old Testament. Similarly, the fact that the Psalter is filled with words *to*, *about*, or *in response to* God means "that the psalms range through the gamut of *experiences* (disaster, war, sickness, exile, celebration, marriage, birth, death) and *emotions* (joy, terror, reflections, gratitude, hate, contentment, depression)."[26] Such crisis moments and feelings occur not in the regular transitional moments of the life cycle (birth,

---

25. Miller, *Interpreting the Psalms*, 11.

26. Miller, *Interpreting the Psalms*, 19.

death, circumcision, wedding, and the like). They occur in the ir-regular moments (the unknown, the unexpected).

The psalms have influenced contemporary faith "liturgically," "devotionally," "pastorally," and "theologically-homiletically." *Liturgically*, the psalms have functioned in differing ways in the worship of both church and synagogue. *Devotionally*, the psalms have been helpful to individuals in varying personal experiences. *Pastorally*, religious leaders have offered the psalms as prayers in situations involving death, grief, sickness, and the like.[27] *Theologically-homiletically*, the psalms inform the faith and life of the congregation through teaching and preaching.[28]

The psalms are timeless. Like the songs in our hymnals, they contain no historical background, which allows them to bridge that gap between the ancient world and the present world probably better than any other book of the Bible. There are two reasons for this: (1) their history is not time bound—it has been the hymnal of both Jews and Christians throughout the ages; (2) their content is not time bound—most of the literature does not relate to any specific period of Israel's history, and thus may reside in any period, then and now. Contrastingly, the psalms do seem time bound in their superscriptions, which were attempts to make connections with other Old Testament events. Such connections, at the very least, offer illustrations of the content of the specific psalms.[29]

The Psalter Challenges Christians

Many individuals and churches read the psalms selectively. How shall Christians understand and use imprecatory psalms (cursing psalms), other than just ignoring or omitting them? What shall be the stance of Christians toward enemies? What does the Psalter teach Christians about forgiveness? What does the Psalter teach Christians about prayer? "Christians have had the tendency to

27. Brueggemann, "Psalms," 4–5.

28. Miller, *Interpreting the Psalms*, 20–21.

29. Miller, *Interpreting the Psalms*, 22.

exclude specific psalms, or specific verses of psalms from their worship."[30] Psalm 137 is a perfect example of this issue. We most often ignore it rather than studying it to learn about how to hate or not hate those who have terribly abused us. Holladay addresses these issues in his chapter on "Censored Texts," in which he cites ten issues faced by Christians who must deal with enemies and would apply the psalms in their lives.[31] (1) Christians are taught to love their enemies (Matt 5:44; Luke 6:27). (2) Christians are instructed to love their enemies in the context of justice, indicating that the triangle of enemies, God, and self are involved. (3) Many times, the psalmists claim they are righteous or innocent, while Psalm 51 and Matt 7:11, Rom 3:23, and 12:3 warn Christians against such claims of self-righteousness. (4) Even so, when Christians find themselves abused, such psalms may offer comfort and empower self-esteem. (5) Oppressed Christians seek vindication, in which such psalms may be helpful (Ps 54). (6) In regard to enemies, Christians should seek reconciliation, or their recognition that they are in the wrong (Ps 31:18). (7) Is it legitimate for Christians to wish harm for their enemies? (8) Could a Christian ever pray for the death of his enemy (137:9)? (9) What of passages that show God's contempt for Israel's enemies (Ps 108:10)? (10) How shall Christians respond when the nation is at war, where in such a case the enemy is the enemy of the nation not the Christian? Holladay concludes the discussion by reaffirming the observation with which he started, "the constant tendency the church has to bypass material with a negative import."[32] So the Psalter is unique among the books of the Bible in the way that it challenges us in our worship, prayer, and attitudes of life.

---

30. Holladay, *Psalms*, 304.

31. Holladay, *Psalms*, 304–13.

32. Holladay, *Psalms*, 314; see also Brueggemann, *Praying*, 44.

Questions for Further Study:
In the Context of Our Epigraphs
Consider the Following Questions

Opening

1. How does knowing that the Psalter was Israel's hymnal (a compilation of five hymnals) help in your understanding of it? Specifically, what does understanding that approximately 50 percent of the psalms are lament psalms, whereas our hymnals have none, indicate to you?

2. What are the implications of the interpretative value of the Hebrew poetry in the Psalter? How can this aid you in your study of the various psalms?

Reflection

1. What is your evaluation of the psalm titles? Are they part of the text or not? What are the implications if they are, or not?

2. How might Christians use the Psalter in ministering to the sick, in counseling and group therapy?

Visualization

1. How does understanding that some of the psalms as *lament-complaint* versus *petitions-supplications* affect the way an individual or congregation prays or worships?

2. How shall we deal with human suffering and prayer in a way that is more like that found in the Psalter?

3. How may we reinterpret today the stereotypical language of such themes as "fearing God," "God as refuge," "the poor," "the afflicted," "God's nearness versus his distance," and the like?

Action

1. Why do people feel more comfortable with the Psalter than other books of the Old Testament?

2. What have you learned about the Psalter that you did not know before this lesson? Make a list of ways these issues may be applied to your Bible study and prayer life.

3. List some ways you might apply your new understanding.

2
___

The Dynamics of Prayer Life

What Happens When We Pray?

Questions regarding Prayer

WHAT IS PRAYER? Is it communication? Is it a *two-way communication*? Is it a *conversation* between individual(s) and God? Is it something we *do* as part of our worship or as part of our daily life? Why do we do it? Does it help us? If so, how does it help us? When we pray, does God really listen? How do we imagine God and ourselves when we pray? Should we really state our true feelings to God, even when those feelings question our faith? For example, "Why, God, did you let this happen?!" Should we bargain with God? That is, should we try to influence God to do what we think is best? Do we really believe we can change God's mind? Under what circumstances is it acceptable to complain to or praise God? What part does God play in our prayers? Does God answer our prayers? If so, when, where, and how does God answer? Do we even expect God to respond to our prayers? These and similar questions you may have pondered within yourself. Perhaps you wanted to discuss them, but were concerned that people might not understand. After all, these questions are not the normal simple questions we consider in Bible classes. They are challenging and seem to indicate that the one posing such a question possesses a weak faith. The opposite is true.

To answer properly these and similar questions, we need to (1) define precisely certain terms and (2) delineate the socio-political-religious motifs found in the psalms as compared to similar motifs in our worship.

Social Reality, Piety, and the I/Thou Relationship

Social reality and piety are the two most significant of these three terms because they affect the third. The definition of social reality in this study is "the basic dynamics of prayer and worship." It is the social setting (the context) in which we pray or worship. Obviously, different religious groups worship in different social realities. More succinctly, we may pose this issue as a question, "What happens to us (spiritually and physically) when we are in the act of praying/worshiping?"

The definition of piety employed in this study derives from Paul Riemann, who defined the term as "the shared perceptions of, attitudes toward, and responses to the divine." Riemann goes on to say, "I say shared, because it is piety as a social-religious phenomenon that I have in mind. In the Psalter we are dealing with a shared piety, the conventional language of the psalms assures us of that."[1] Therefore, Riemann's definition of piety includes social reality. Specifically, when we are worshiping or praying privately, how do we perceive, think, or imagine God? The same goes for corporate worship. When we worship corporately as Christians, "how do we perceive, think, or imagine God?" This is piety (whether worship is personal or public), whereas social reality is the dynamics of the worship setting (whether social or private).

I/Thou employs Martin Buber's book title[2] (with a modified definition); I use this term to refer to how we perceive ourselves in our relationship to God. Individually, we may have one view, while

---

1. Riemann, *Dissonant Pieties*, 57.
2. Buber, *I and Thou*.

corporately we may have another view. The individual I/Thou may be different from the corporate I/Thou (we/you) and we may not even be aware of it. However, the "I" and the "Thou" must be imagined together. This I/Thou relationship focuses awareness on who we really are, without any facades, and shapes the sense of what is self-evidently true. The disruption of this relationship creates a crisis for the pious person, who will then attempt to bring these two back into alignment. Isaiah 6 illustrates this dynamic. There Isaiah had a vision of the Lord sitting on his throne. The seraphs cried, "Holy, holy, holy is the LORD of hosts; the whole earth is full of his glory!" (v. 3 NRSV). Chapters 1–5, record Isaiah's sermons of condemnation focusing on Israel's sins. However, in his vision, he came face-to-face with the Lord. This new experience, this new social reality, greatly affected his piety and his understanding of his I/Thou relationship; he recognized the change in his relationship with God and responded in v. 5, "Woe is me! I am lost; for I am a man of unclean lips, and I live among people of unclean lips; yet my eyes have seen the King, the LORD of hosts!" (NRSV). No longer did Isaiah see Israel as the problem. Having seen God, Isaiah recognized that *he* was part of the problem! Like Isaiah, when we come to see ourselves as God sees us, we see ourselves as we really are and we should attempt to correct and improve our relationship to him (our I/Thou) by doing whatever is necessary to ensure that our relationship to him continues. Sadly, however, this is not always the case. Often church problems arise when individuals, like Isaiah, realize their piety and social reality are incongruent. Instead of making needed adjustments in their piety they either attempt to shift the blame to someone else and/or change their social reality. To illustrate, a church that observed the Lord's Supper every Sunday planned to build a new sanctuary. The church instructed the architect to design the sanctuary in a way that would promote improvement in their worship services. When he asked what was the most important reason for their worship, they responded, "We come together to worship on Sunday to observe the Lord's Supper; that is the most important thing we do." The architect designed a round sanctuary with seats lining the walls. In the middle was the

Lord's Table. The church was very indignant and asked, "What is this?" The architect replied, "You said the most important reason for your coming together was your focus on the Lord's Supper. This blueprint helps you focus on that." They replied, "That is the most ludicrous thing we ever heard! Everyone knows that a sanctuary should have a stage upon which sits a pulpit, with a baptistry behind it. The Lord's Table should be in front facing the pews that fill the sanctuary!" What was wrong? In terms of the church's piety, they believed the main reason they came together was to worship in their observance of the Lord's Supper, when actually they engaged in a number of other worship activities. Futher, the architect's blueprint forced the church to see that their social reality was very passive. Whoever was on the stage was in charge, while the audience for the most part was passive. Piously they believed they were doing one thing, while in terms of their worship activities they were doing something else. Instead of following Isaiah's example and recognizing their inconsistency, they chose to shift the blame to the architect. This set of circumstances causes many church problems because the individuals involved who piously believe they are doing one thing become very disturbed and blame others when someone points out their social reality is contradictory to their piety. So, understanding these issues should help us improve in our worship practices and beliefs if we are willing to recognize our mistaken ideas, as did Isaiah.

Our Social Reality, Piety, and I/Thou Compared to the Psalter's Piety

Metaphorically speaking, what occurs in the Psalter occurs in the church. Granted, we live in a different world than the people of the Psalter. Yet, being human, when we pray to God, we have the same feelings, attitudes, doubts, and strengths the psalmists had. This means a better understanding of the social reality, piety, and I/Thou in psalms can help us understand the same in our lives and worship.

To accomplish this, we must ask two important questions. First, "What are the central areas of religious concern in the Psalter?" The psalms do not focus explicitly on transitional moments in the life cycle, for example, birth, circumcision, transition from adolescence to adulthood, marriage, or death. For example, the only mention of a wedding is one about a king (Ps 45). Instead, the psalms focus on irregular crisis moments that occur in our lives— the things that are unexpected. Therefore, various psalms deal with the religious needs of groups or individuals at those unforeseen points where they are most analogous to us. At the same time, they are least distinguished when identifying the specific crisis or crises they faced. This is because, as we noted in the previous lesson, the language is so general the reader often cannot determine the precise issues affecting the psalmist. Yet this general language makes vivid the situation as it was. Like songs in hymnals, they become adaptable to each person's specific needs for edification, encouragement.

The second question, "How would one characterize the fundamental religious attitudes in the Psalter?" begins to focus on the significant part of the I/Thou relationship. It reaches the deepest human needs and most profound fears, which are extant today as they were in Israel and the ancient Near East. As we shall see in the next lesson, but only illustrate generally here, the psalmists did not assume their views and God's views had to agree. They perceived themselves as negotiating with God to change God's mind regarding their situations. In doing so, they were frank and open. Always respectful, they often approached God in a way that may shock many Christians. Indeed, this attitude exists outside the Psalter. In 1 Samuel 1, Hannah prayed for a son. Her prayer, however, took on the structure of a bargain. The bargaining element of her prayer demonstrates her social reality, piety, and her sense of I/Thou. In 1 Sam 1:11, Hannah vowed,

> 'O LORD of hosts, if only you will look on the misery of your servant, and not forget your servant, but will give to your servant a male child, then I will set him before you as a nazirite until the day of his death. He shall drink

neither wine nor intoxicants, and no razor shall touch his head'" (NRSV).

Note her prayer, which begins in v. 10, contains this vow. Specifically, her bargain proposed to God was, "God, if you will give me a son, I will give him back to you." Similarly, Jacob when fleeing Esau demonstrated his talent as an excellent bargainer. In his proposed bargain with God in Gen 28:20–22, Jacob offers six obligations for God and only three obligations for himself! For clarity, God's obligations are in italic font while Jacob's are in bold font.

> *If God will be with me* and will *keep me in this way that I go*, and will *give me bread to eat* and *clothing to wear*, so that *I come again to my father's house in peace*, then **the LORD shall be my God**, and **this stone . . . shall be God's house**. And of *all that you give me* **I will give a full tenth to you**. (NRSV)

Neither Jacob nor Hannah had any difficulty expressing what they thought they needed. Their piety seems to indicate they could forthrightly take their needs to God in prayer, that God was a God with whom one could bargain, and that fundamentally they expected a response from God to their proposals. In both cases, the subsequent events showed these ideas (faith?) were in fact correct.

We will explore these issues in more detail later. For now, the most important questions are the ones we asked at the beginning of this lesson, but with the added question, "Now that we have surveyed the general nature of these issues, have your answers to the questions first proposed changed; if so, how and why?"

Questions for Further Study: In the Context of Our Epigraphs Consider the Following Questions

Opening

1. What is prayer? Is it communication? Is it a two-way communication? Is it a conversation between individual(s) and

God? Is it something we *do* as part of our worship or as part of our daily life?

2. Why do we do it? Does it help us? If so, how does it help us?

Reflection

1. When we pray, does God really listen? How do we *see* God and ourselves when we pray?

2. Should we really state our true feelings to God, even when those feelings are feelings that question our faith? For example, "Why God did you let this happen?!"

Visualization

1. Should we bargain with God? That is, should we try to influence God to do what we think is best?

2. Do we really believe we can change God's mind?

Action

1. Under what circumstances is it acceptable to complain to or praise God?

2. What part does God play in our prayers? Does God answer our prayers? If so, when, where, and how does God answer? Do we even expect God to respond to our prayers?

3. This week, as you pray, attempt to be bolder in your prayers, whether asking for things you need, informing God of your concerns, or thanking God for blessings he has sent your way.

4. How do you think you should pray such prayers?

3

The Impact of the Social Reality, Piety, and I/Thou of the Psalter versus That of John Calvin on the Christian's Prayer Life

Social Reality and Piety of the Psalter

THE PSALTER CONTAINS MATERIAL of self-importance that makes us feel uncomfortable. Seldom does it picture God as a parent as we do. Such occurrences appear in the Royal Psalms, which designate someone (usually God's anointed, Ps 2) as "God's son." Therefore, while we call God "Father," to the psalmists he was God. Rather, than understanding of God as provider, there is a sense of give-and-take between claimant and God. Compare Ps 80:18–19,

> Then we shall not turn back from you;
> give us life, and we will call on your name!
> Restore us, O LORD God of hosts;
> let your face shine, that we may be saved! (NRSV)

The psalmists do not approach humbly and contritely. Rather there is a sense of bargaining. Neither is there the willingness to confess wrongs, but a sense of questioning why God has forgotten, hidden from, and exhibited wrath toward the plaintiff. Compare Ps 88:12–18,

> 12 Are your wonders known in the darkness,
> or your saving help in the land of forgetfulness?
> 13 But I, O LORD, cry out to you;
> in the morning my prayer comes before you.
> 14 O LORD, why do you cast me off?
> Why do you hide your face from me?
> 15 Wretched and close to death from my youth up,
> I suffer your terrors; I am desperate.
> 16 Your wrath has swept over me;
> your dread assaults destroy me.
> 17 They surround me like a flood all day long;
> from all sides they close in on me.
> 18 You have caused friend and neighbor to shun me;
> my companions are in darkness. (NRSV)

Few complaint psalms acknowledge sin and ask forgiveness. Rather, as in Ps 79:8–9, the supplicants request that God make atonement.

> 8 Do not remember against us the iniquities of our ancestors;
> let your compassion come speedily to meet us,
> for we are brought very low.
> 9 Help us, O God of our salvation,
> for the glory of your name;
> deliver us, and forgive our sins,
> for your name's sake. (NRSV)

They even go so far as to point out that the obligation really falls with God, as Ps 74:1 illustrates,

> O God, why do you cast us off forever?
> Why does your anger smoke against the sheep of your pasture?

Sometimes the petitioner really says that God has neglected him, as demonstrated in Ps 22:1.

> My God, my God, why have you forsaken me?
> Why are you so far from helping me, from the words of my groaning? (NRSV)

These examples strikingly illustrate that the authors of the complaint psalms felt they were living in a hostile environment and surrounded by enemies. These petitioners' vulnerability drives their anxiety. Yet, at other times, they seem very self-assured. How do we understand these differences? Note the contrasting views found in Psalm 56. Though reeling from his enemies's attacks, afraid, and facing strife and harm, the psalmist interspaces the first part of the psalm with voices of confidence, as if he is encouraging himself, until by the end of the psalm he seems convinced that God has heard his prayer and everything will work out.

1 Be gracious to me, O God, for people trample on me;
  all day long foes oppress me;
2 my enemies trample on me all day long,
  for many fight against me.
O Most High, 3 when I am afraid,
  I put my trust in you.
4 In God, whose word I praise,
  in God I trust; I am not afraid;
  what can flesh do to me?
5 All day long they seek to injure my cause;
  all their thoughts are against me for evil.
6 They stir up strife, they lurk,
  they watch my steps.
As they hoped to have my life,
  7 so repay them for their crime;
  in wrath cast down the peoples, O God!
8 You have kept count of my tossings;
  put my tears in your bottle.
  Are they not in your record?
9 Then my enemies will retreat
  in the day when I call.
  This I know, that God is for me.
10 In God, whose word I praise,
  in the LORD, whose word I praise,
11 in God I trust; I am not afraid.
  What can a mere mortal do to me?
12 My vows to you I must perform, O God;
  I will render thank offerings to you.
13 For you have delivered my soul from death,
  and my feet from falling,
so that I may walk before God
  in the light of life.

Such statements of confidence scholars have dubbed the "certainty of hearing." These seem to suggest the petitioner believes God has heard his prayer, in much the same manner as Hannah's experience in 1 Samuel 1–2, or serve as self-encouragement in the middle of the trial.

Even when praising God for answered previous prayers, the psalmists approached him boldly. Psalm 30 is a very good example. In this thanksgiving-praise psalm; the psalmist praises and thanks God for answering his former prayer. We do not know many details of that prayer, but v. 9 contains the specific motivational statement for God to answer his request. Phrasing the prayer in the form of a rhetorical question (from the psalmist's point of view), he says, "What profit is there in my death, if I go down to the Pit? Will the dust praise you? Will it tell of your faithfulness?" Now, think about this for a moment. If you were dying but believed that if you prayed fervently and asked God to spare your life he might do so, what would you pray? Would you pray, as this psalmist did, a rhetorical question whose point was something like, "You need to let me live, because if I die, I will not be around to praise you or tell others of your faithfulness"? When I read this verse then read Heb 4:14–16 and its admonition to "approach the throne of grace with boldness, so that we may receive mercy and find grace to help in time of need" (NRSV), I have difficulty understanding what the Hebrews writer is saying. The Greek word *parrēsí* has a range of meanings: (1) "a use of speech that conceals nothing and passes over nothing, *outspokenness, frankness, plainness*"; and (2) "a state of boldness and confidence, *courage, confidence, boldness, fearlessness*."[1] Specifically, if Ps 30:9 does not portray a bold approach to God, what is the boldness the Hebrews writer is speaking about?

By way of summary, the people praying in the Psalter were real people. They experienced similar problems to those you and I have, and they furnish examples for us in our prayer lives. They realized and acknowledged adversity and misfortune in the universe. To these people there was often a sense of resignation

1. BDAG, 781–82.

and a sense of acceptance versus rejection in their personal lives. Ideals such as loyalty and trustworthiness were paramount. They believed that if God could impose such personal pressures on them, then the reverse was also true. They believed they could put similar counter-pressures on God; they did not hold back. Specifically, "they do not feel they must submit humbly and penitently to whatever God ordains. There is always the possibility that God can be persuaded—or provoked, if it comes to that—to change course and act on their behalf. The future may still be open, the final decision not yet made."[2]

John Calvin's Social Reality and Piety Reflected a Marked Contrast

Calvin's emphasis of the sovereignty of God caused him to anticipate the question, "But someone will say, does God not know . . . , both in what respect we are troubled and what is expedient for us, so that it may seem superfluous that he should be stirred up by our prayers . . . [The Lord] ordained it not so much for his own sake as for ours."[3] Calvin's answer to this question contained six reasons for us to pray. (1) *Prayer creates zeal in us*: "that our hearts may be fired with a zealous and burning desire ever to seek, love, and serve him." (2) *Prayer awakens honorable desires and kills dishonorable desires*: "there may enter our hearts no desire and no wish . . . of which we should be ashamed . . . , while we learn to set all our wishes before his eyes." (3) *Prayer makes us grateful*: "that we be prepared to receive his benefits with true gratitude of heart and thanksgiving." (4) *Prayer causes us to meditate on God's kindness*: "having ordained what we were seeking, and . . . convinced that he has answered our prayers, we should be led to meditate upon his kindness." (5) *Prayer makes us thankful for answered prayers*: "we embrace . . . those things which we acknowledge to be obtained by prayers." (6) *Prayer establishes our faith in God's providence*: "that

2. Riemann, *Dissonant Pieties*, 60–61.

3. Calvin, *Institutes*, 3.20.3.

use and experience may . . . confirm his providence, while we understand . . . that he promises never to fail us."[4]

Calvin also issued four rules for acceptable prayer. (1) *We should pray with reverence*, describing prayer as a "conversation with God" in which the one praying must frame the "prayer duly and properly" and not be "distracted by wandering thoughts." (2) *We should pray with a sense of want and penitence*, in which we should "sense our own insufficiency," while "pondering how we need all we seek." (3) *We should pray humbly, yielding all confidence in ourselves*, for anyone who prays to God should pray "in his humility giving glory completely to God," and "put away all self-assurance." (4) *We should pray with the confident hope of success in our prayers*, believing "that our prayers will be answered."[5]

Taken together, Calvin believed the purpose of prayer is to bring the supplicant's feelings in line with God's sovereignty, particularly his predestination and foreknowledge. Granted, when one thinks about approaching God in prayer, things like reverence, humility, and repentance, coupled with confidence, should come into play. In fact, we often seem to focus so much on reverence, humility, and repentance that we fail to explore the meaning of confidence and boldness in our approach to God. Because Calvin's ideas about prayer were rooted in his understanding of God's sovereignty as revealed in his predestination and foreknowledge, he was driven to the conclusion that since God had already predestined everything that happens, and, consequently, already knows what is going to happen, prayers are a way to realign a person's feelings with what God predestined and foreknew. Many today pray in similar fashion and express similar views. Such ideas set the stage for prayers that are based on the view that our prayers do not change God's mind, but serve as experiences to align our will with God's predestination and foreknowledge.

However, comparisons of Calvin's views with those expressed by the author of Psalm 30 indicate that the psalmist's social reality and piety in prayer were quite different. For example, he does not

4. Calvin, *Institutes*, 3.20.3.

5. Calvin, *Institutes*, 3:20:4–14.

consider repentance. He phrases his petition unconditionally. He does not moralize about why God changed his mind. He very self-importantly states that if he died he would cease to praise God. The implication is that God needed him. Therefore, there is quite a difference in views and purpose of prayer between Calvin and those expressed in Psalm 30.

From the above, we may observe that the psalmist believed his prayer changed God's mind, which points to some general observations. First, the various psalms did not take it for granted that human interests and divine interests agree. Second, there was a keen sense of conflicting interests, which can only be resolved through negotiation. Third, the gulf between the human and the divine is real. Fourth, the petitioners prayed for a change in their welfare. Fifth, they realize that they often approach a line of rebelliousness. As Riemann very articulately expresses it,

> Their sense of what is appropriate in prayer has remarkably little in common with the one set forth in Calvin's rules. They revel in spirited engagement with God rather than devout resignation. Their complaints are typically very direct, even feisty. They often speak as though God were part of the problem, as Psalm 39 does when it asks God to "look away"—Calvin's parade example of unlawful petition. When they do so, they can be indignant, reproachful and even bitingly ironic. On the other hand, they do not regard it as improper to be ingratiating and proffer inducements. They can represent themselves as helpless and pitiful, or put forward a claim of unshakable confidence and trust, and often do both together. They know what it is to beg forgiveness, but they do not do so every time they find themselves in trouble. They present themselves to God more often as victims rather than as sinners. And when they cry to be delivered from their troubles and those who trouble them, they look for deliverance and nothing less; they do not pray for patience and fortitude to bear it, or concede the outcome in advance by deferring to God's sovereign will or superior judgment.[6]

6. Riemann, *Dissonant Pieties*, 59.

Christians' Social Reality, Piety, and I/Thou Today Seem More in Agreement with John Calvin than the Psalms

Note the following example questions and statements of Christians, which reflect more Calvin's view than those of the Psalter. (1) "Why pray at all if God knows everything?" (2) "Not my will, but God's will must be done!" This and similar statements often come after quoting the "b" part of Jesus' petition, "yet, not my will but yours be done" (Luke 22:42b NRSV). Students of this passage often omit the "a" part of the statement, where Jesus is attempting to change God's mind! "Father, if you are willing, remove this cup from me" (NRSV). Christians may exhibit this imbalance due to a fear of not doing God's will; a fear whose overemphasis creates the tendency to overlook that Jesus' example shows God's willingness to hear our supplications.

These expressed attitudes and interpretations raise the question, "Is prayer just an exercise for us to get our feelings and thoughts in line with God's will (Calvin), or do we really believe that our prayers matter, that we can change God's mind (the psalmists)?" If the answer is, "We need to align our feelings with God because God knows all things," then we pray more like Calvin than the psalmists. For those of us who find ourselves in this situation, there exist several reasons for this Calvinistic approach to prayer.

First, the church's social reality and piety, relative to prayer and worship, have given, perhaps unknowingly, credence to Calvin's approach. Based on his personal experiences, Balentine has made several astute and disturbing observations. Public prayers, though reflective, and seemingly spontaneous, are offered with a "certain sameness." Regardless of who prays, the prayers petition God to "bless, heal, forgive, direct, in accordance with the divine will," in which they exhibit a submissive attitude, and acknowledge humanity's dependence on God's sovereignty and humanity's dependence on God. These are primarily prayers of submission, but are "woefully irrelevant." This is because the supplicants understand that they must "praise God, but not protest" and "petition

God, but not interrogate" him. Instead, they should accept and submit to the "incomprehensible will of God," and "never challenge or rebel." Balentine then raises these provocative questions, "'You must not question God.' If one cannot question God, then to whom does one direct the questions? If God is a God whom we cannot question, then what kind of God is this to whom we are committing ourselves?" He notes the church has taught people both "how to pray" as well as "how not to pray." It has taught participants "how to pray" by encouraging them "to be optimistic," to "be hopeful in expectation of redemption and deliverance," and "to embrace and encourage probes, wonderments, and questions about life's purpose, and about God, only within contexts carefully calculated not to leave the answer in doubt." It has taught its members "how not to pray" by maintaining "a level of non-engagement with hurt and doubt that threatens to rob life in relation to God of its vitality and honesty."[7]

Neither does Balentine allow the academy to escape his criticism. It too has failed by ignoring such themes in the wisdom literature and psalms, leaving the impression that the literature "speaks in tones of praise and thankfulness for divine order and providential care."[8] Balentine authored *Prayers of the Hebrew Bible* in 1993. While true then, scholarship has made much progress in this area in the ensuing years. There is still much to do, because pastors, preachers, and other church leaders, though trained in the academic appreciation of the biblical material, are often unqualified in these areas most needed by the church. Scholarship needs to continue to seek ways to bridge this gap.[9] This study is one such attempt. In lesson 4 we will explore these issues in more detail and offer some possible ways to improve our prayer lives.

---

7. Balentine, *Prayer*, 3–6.

8. Balentine, *Prayer*, 7.

9. Balentine, *Prayer*, 6–7.

Questions for Further Study:
In the Context of Our Epigraphs
Consider the Following Questions

Opening

1. Do you see a significant difference between the examples of the psalmists and Calvin in their approach to prayer?

2. Why do you think these differences occur?

Reflection

1. Which makes you feel more comfortable, Calvin, or the psalmists?

2. Which makes you feel more uncomfortable, Calvin, or the psalmists?

Visualization

1. Do you think you pray more like the psalmists or Calvin?

2. Can you imagine the results should you attempt to pray more like the psalmists?

3. What would you specifically ask?

Action

1. This week, attempt to pray like the psalmists.

2. Do you feel uncomfortable praying in this manner, and if you do, why do you suppose that is the case?

3. What hindrances would keep you from praying in this manner? Are they valid self-criticisms?

4

A Better Understanding of God Equals Improvement in Social Reality, Piety, and Prayer

Introduction

WE SAW IN THE last lesson that many Christians tend to pray more in line with the piety of John Calvin than that portrayed in the Psalter. One of the reasons for this is the foundational issue of perception. How we perceive people and our assumptions about them form the core of how we speak and interact with them. This situation is no different in our relationships with God. How we conceive of God and our fundamental assumptions about him (piety) inform our faith and our relationship to him. Therefore, this piety influences the way we pray to and worship him. This lesson explores these issues to highlight how they affect our prayer life and worship. Specifically, to have a more perfect prayer life we must develop better understanding of God's relationship to humanity, the world, and the church's responsibility.

How Do God and Humanity Relate?

Balentine discusses how the Old Testament employs "anthropomorphic metaphors" to describe God when describing the divine-human relationship in prayer. For Balentine, these represent a "dialogue between God and humanity."[1] Here I focus on how anthropomorphic metaphors stand in contrast to the systematic theological approach (adhered to by most Christians) that attempts to describe God by listing his major characteristics and synthesizing them through a reading of the biblical text, though they are not biblical terms at all. Three such examples are *omniscience, omnipresence,* and *omnipotence*; all three, respectively, referring to God's knowledge, presence in the world, and power. However, a careful reading of the Bible shows it often reads in ways that seem to illustrate that these theological terms do not fit. This is so although other passages seem to prove their veracity. Yes, there are passages that illustrate these systematic theological descriptions. However, there are other passages that seem to say God is not omniscient, and the like. One such example is Gen 6:6, "And the LORD was sorry that he had made humankind on the earth, and it grieved him to his heart" (NRSV). Now, in systematic-theological terms, since God is omniscient, then he should not have been sorry he created man, because he would have known this would occur. Similarly, Gen 11:5 observes about the Tower of Babel, "The LORD came down to see the city and the tower, which mortals had built" (NRSV), describing God in a way that seems to indicate he is neither omniscient nor omnipresent.

Our systematic-theological approach encourages us to reconcile ideas of the omniscience and omnipresence of God with these differing descriptions by saying that Gen 6:6 and 11:5 are anthropomorphic descriptions of God; simply put, we imply that God is so indescribable that we must explain him by assigning him human characteristics. An interesting aside here is that we never state what this interpretation explains about God in these cases. Saying Gen 6:6 is a statement that God "was sorry" he had made man still does nothing to describe God. Interpretatively, this anthropomorphism is worthless in any useful or practical way. It confuses our understanding of God's character rather than explaining it. A similar thing occurs in Gen 11:5. Saying that God "came down to

---

1. Balentine, *Prayer*, 37.

see the city and the tower" (NRSV) of Babel, confuses our view of God rather than clarifying it. What does the phrase "came down to see" add to our understanding of the sin of the Tower of Babel and God's relationship to that event, and his attributes? Again, the anthropomorphism does not explain how this helps understand God's attributes.

The example of Exodus 32 is a more specific illustration of how our piety, when using non-biblical terms such as omniscience, creates more problems, and fails us in prayer. Israel created the golden calf, in response to which God told Moses, "Now let me alone, so that my wrath may burn hot against them and I may consume them; and of you I will make a great nation" (v. 10 NRSV). However, vv. 11–13 report that Moses prayed and argued with God not to take those actions. Verse 14 records, "And the LORD changed his mind about the disaster that he had planned to bring on his people" (NRSV). The fact that God "changed his mind" creates a problem for our preconceived, pious belief in God's omniscience (a specific piety), because "if God know everything, then he knew before Moses would pray that Moses would pray, he knew what Moses would pray, and he knew the results of that prayer." Therefore, when God said he was going to destroy Israel in v. 10, he knew Moses' prayer would cause him to change his mind and he would not destroy them. Such a conclusion, influenced by the a priori belief and interpretation of an omniscient God, would mean that God lied to Moses! We cannot accept that. This results in many individuals' idea that they cannot change God's mind with their prayers, because God already knows the outcome. A less-known example is Jer 7:31. There Jeremiah states that the evil the people were enacting in "building the high place of Topheth" and burning "their sons and their daughters in the fire" was something "I did not command, nor did it come into my mind" (NRSV). Either that is a true statement or anthropomorphic hyperbole to attempt to communicate how much the people shocked God by the depths to which they would go. However, like Genesis 6, such anthropomorphic interpretation does not work, because it does not illustrate anything about God's character. This discussion of the extent of

God's knowledge is not primary here. In fact, we could explore many deeper issues; however, to do so would shift our focus away from understanding how our piety needs some adjustments. We do not have to provide answers for everything, we need only believe. Simply stated, I believe God "was sorry" he made man in Gen 6:6. I believe he did go down to see the tower of Babel. Further, I believe Moses' prayer changed God's mind in Exodus 32. I believe Israel did some things God had not conceived of before in Jer 7:31. Am I able to explain these verses completely? No, but I do not have to do so as systematic theology demands. Rather in simple faith, I must humbly believe that the God we worship is so much the "Great Other" from us, that I doubt I could understand these things if he explained them. This discussion shows we spend far too much time attempting to reconcile and give answers to things we will never completely understand or answer, when the simpler, more important, thing to do is believe.

How Does God Relate to the World?

Quite naturally, Balentine next moves into a general discussion of God's relationship with the created world, noting among other things that God's residence in heaven does not separate him from our residence here on earth. In this created order, God either relates to time or does not relate to time as past, present, and future.[2] I would like here to explore the practical and philosophical issues this relatedness creates as we attempt to pray more like the psalmists. If God does not relate to time as past, present, and future, then there is no place for contingencies brought about by divine-human communication (prayer). Consequently, the supplicant is unable to persuade God to take an appropriate course of action. This results in prayer like Calvin's, which is merely an exercise to bring our thoughts, minds, feelings, and emotions in line with what God has already predetermined or foreknown. If God relates to time as past, present, and future, there is a place for contingencies, in

2. Balentine, *Prayer*, 38–47.

which, through divine-human communication (prayer) the supplicant can persuade God to take an appropriate course of action. To illustrate, we must make numerous choices in life. Some of these are of little consequence. "Shall I purchase gas at this station or another?" "Shall I shop at this store or another?" "Shall I participate in this activity today or put it off?" We make these decisions almost automatically, depending upon our schedule that day and some other, minor issue. Other decisions will affect our future greatly. "Shall I marry, and if so, whom?" "Shall we have children?" "Shall I take this job?" In this context, the real questions are, "What are our presuppositions (our pieties) about God's part in these decisions?" "Do we believe future answers are left open depending upon whether and how we pray about them?" "How do we expect God to answer our prayers?" "Are the answers to these questions already mapped out?" "Is prayer just an exercise to help us bend our will to what God has already determined or foreknows?" "When we pray these prayers, are we looking for answers for requests or are we waiting to figure out what God wants us to do so we can bend our wills to his?" Put simply, "How do we expect God to answer our prayers?"

A personal example may help to demonstrate the issue. Several years ago, I was in discussion with a very godly preacher friend who was considering moving to another church's offered employment. This man had such a wonderful relationship with the congregation where he preached that, when he received the offer to move to another congregation, he approached his leaders and advised them of the opportunity. These leaders not only encouraged him to do what was best for him and his family, but also made that same announcement to the congregation, saying basically, "Our Brother has received an opportunity to move to another congregation. We would love for him to decide to remain with us, but we also want what is best for him and his family. We ask that you pray for him and his family that the best decision will be made in accordance with God's providence." You can imagine how the congregation flooded the man and his family with well-intentioned advice. One night at a church bowling party, I addressed the issue.

I said, "Brother, I am sure people are giving you plenty of advice and encouragement," and that I was willing to put in my "two-cents-worth" if he was interested. When he said he was interested, I asked, "If you go, will you attempt to do God's will and will God bless you?" He replied, "Yes." I asked, "If you stay, will you attempt to do God's will and will he bless you?" He replied, "Yes." I asked, "Then why don't you stop asking God what he wants you to do and either go or stay? Maybe God is asking, 'Do you want a Snickers or a Three Musketeers?' Maybe God does not really care whether you go or stay, but is offering you an opportunity depending upon the decision you make." This story illustrates how we often focus so much on wanting to do God's will that we paralyze ourselves waiting for some sign of his will. Doing God's will should be a given. Such prayers, in my view, are more like Calvin's than the psalmists' and waste our time. Where these and similar views occur among us, we must change this piety thereby opening greater possibilities for the divine-human dialogue, both publicly and privately.

Consideration of these issues influenced me to modify my piety regarding God's will and prayer. I now perceive that prayer and God's will for my life are more like a game of checkers or chess with God. After struggling and thinking diligently, I move my piece on the board. God immediately moves his piece and says, "Your move!" Foundational to this image is the belief, "I plan to do God's will." That does not change. However, when given life's choices, I now pray for wisdom (Jas 1:5), then I seek advice of godly people, then I make my decision. I no longer ask God, "What is your will for me in this?" I go forward in the confidence that if I make a good decision, God's blessing will follow. If I make a bad decision, God will give me experiences that teach me to see my error and change my focus and actions, thereby providing for the growing of my faith and wisdom. Viewed this way, there are no bad decisions. They produce either happier or sadder situations, but God acts according to the decision I have made to fit me in with his plans for what is best for my family, the church, the world, and me (Rom 8:28).

Such experiences as the conversation with my preacher friend illustrate that for many of us our discomfort with complaint/lament, as well as our failure to reconcile our definition of God's omnipotence, omniscience, and the like, has greatly weakened our prayer life and worship. This imprecise piety creates an atmosphere in which many feel uncomfortable expressing their feelings boldly to God. Such thoughts and prayers, like the lament psalms, "lead us into dangerous acknowledgment of how life really is" and "into the presence of God where everything is not polite and civil."[3] Still others in their heart of hearts wonder just how God answers prayers, since he knows already what we are going to pray, and how he will answer it. These views reduce prayer to an exercise like Calvin's prayer piety. People who wonder such things are often afraid to voice them because they believe complaint is sinful and to ask whether God knows everything is something that Christians should not discuss. We need to engage in Bible study that results in our recognition that we are attempting to understand God, something never completely attainable, but something toward which we must continually strive. Being more biblical in our descriptions, while humbly recognizing that we do not need to understand everything about these issues but just believe what the text says, is a far more exciting way to live our lives before God.

The Church's Improved Social Reality, Piety, and Prayer

Many readers may remember hearing of or participating in prayer services at the church building. We do not hear that term much anymore. In fact, I cannot remember ever attending a prayer service or prayer meeting as a child. It was always "mid-week Bible Study," or "Wednesday Night Bible Study," or the like. In short, I never experienced the church coming together just to pray.

Several years ago, I made this observation while doing a Psalms and Prayer Workshop where I presented this material. The

---

3. Brueggemann, *Message*, 53.

leaders decided to begin meeting on Sunday an hour before the evening services and having a prayer service or prayer meeting before the evening worship. That congregation decided to divide into a men's group and a women's group. Each group created a list about what they believed they needed to pray, and then spent that hour in prayer before the evening worship. The fact that many of us have not experienced such services is a further indication that we need to give more serious attention to public and private prayers, and that the Psalter is the perfect model for us in this venue.

The church must identify itself as a house of prayer, which brings together God and the community. Doing so creates a primary ministry of ongoing dialogue and communion with God through prayer.[4] Balentine goes on to note several key areas the church must address if it is to improve its mission. I would argue they must become the foundational beliefs of individual supplicants in prayer and thanksgiving. If the individual supplicants can agree on this piety and demonstrate it in its public social reality in worship, then the church will have a greater affect in its mission of bringing people to the Lord. Note these issues. (1) We must recognize God for what he is while being free to question his actions. (2) We must become more at ease with radical dialogue, which itself exhibits a close relationship. (3) We must recognize the open-endedness of life questioning, emphasizing the dialogue of prayer. (4) We must be willing to take up the cause of the victim, affirming that God sides with the victim. (5) We must recognize the risks of lament. In short, lament is unmanageable—not popular to the masses who will possibly seek answers elsewhere. (6) We must recognize the danger of lament because it involves questioning which may alter faith,[5] as the song "Where Could I Go but to the Lord" implies.

Praise is opposite from lament and affirms that we are truly in need of God. If we do not praise we will relapse into conceit and the focus will shift from God to the idolatry of self. Jeremiah's temple sermon (Jer 7:1–15; 26:1–14) illustrates this. Jeremiah's

---

4. Balentine, *Prayers*, 274–75.

5 Balentine, *Prayer*, 287–95. For the song's lyrics and brief biography of the author, see https://hymnary.org/text/living_below_in_this_old_sinful_world.

audience reveled in their praise of God as his people, while continually engaging in disobedience.[6] In this state, they continually called to mind how God had spared the people and the temple in the days of Hezekiah, reflecting the false idea that God would save them again. They *knew* they were God's covenant people and thought they had evidence of God's protection in the past. Therefore, they said, "This is the temple of the LORD, the temple of the LORD, the temple of the LORD" (Jer 7:4 NRSV). They praised God for being his people and practicing their religion, but lived wickedly. Sometimes today, we see the same thing. Christians worship correctly, but live wickedly. If Jeremiah were to preach to such people today he would probably say something like, "Do not trust in these deceptive words: 'The Church, the Church, the Church.'" He would direct that sermon to people who are religious but live wicked lives. Such people practice tradition more than obedience. Further, such statements are acceptable only if they derive from honest hearts that practice only biblical traditions. We should call any tradition that is not biblical into question. The church must engage in prayer that keeps God in the community and continues to work in the world.[7] These issues create the need to begin with the Psalter. If we learn how to improve the social reality and piety of our prayer life through a study of the piety of the psalmists, we may open new areas of application, even beyond those listed above by Balentine. This improved understanding of prayer psalms will improve the social reality and piety in our prayer life. Then we will begin to practice better Phil 4:6–7, resulting in our finally reaching the "peace of God." Having laid this foundation, we will explore in the next lessons how we may use the lament and praise psalms of the Psalter as a model for our prayers.

---

6. Balentine, *Prayers*, 279–80.

7. Balentine, *Prayer*, 273.

Questions for Further Study:
In the Context of Our Epigraphs
Consider the Following Questions

Opening

1. What is your piety? That is, how do you perceive God? What are your perceptions' major characteristics? How do these specifically affect the way you pray?

2. How do you believe God relates to the world? Are you comfortable thinking of God in theological but not biblical terms (e.g., omniscience, omnipotence, and omnipresence)? Are you comfortable with passages that imply God does not know everything (like Gen 6:6 and Jer 7:31), or passages that seem to indicate God is not omnipresent (like Gen 11:7)? Do you feel you must explain such statements in terms of anthropomorphisms, or are you comfortable accepting such statements even though you cannot explain them?

Reflection

1. How do you think your understanding of the foreknowledge of God affects your views of prayer? If you believe God knows everything, how does this affect your prayer life? How do you explain God changing his mind regarding the destruction of Israel, though he told Moses he would destroy the nation in Exodus 32?

2. How do you believe God relates to the world? Do you believe God has left some decisions to you and that he will make appropriate adjustments according to your decisions, or do you believe God already has everything mapped out and that your prayers are just spiritual exercises? In short, is there a place in your prayer life to believe God may be

placing options before you and waiting for you to choose, or is this a foreign idea to you?

Visualization

1. Can you imagine attending a true prayer service, where a group or the church met to do nothing but pray about situations and events that were important to them? What do you think would be the implications of your congregation organized such meetings?

2. In such a service, do you think you would be comfortable or uncomfortable with lament?

3. Why do you think the church's hymnals have no songs of lament in them? Can you describe the imbalance created because the church's hymnals contain only praise and edification songs, and no songs of lament?

4. What do you think would be the impact if we as individuals and as congregations became more comfortable with lament, which would create a greater balance in our piety and social reality due to our practice of both?

Action

1. Conduct a family or friend's prayer meeting in which you attempt to apply both praise and lament. Pray explicitly for issues in which you would like God to intervene. Then look to see how he intervened. Make a note of these.

2. Later in the week, have a second prayer meeting with your family or friends in which you thank/praise God for his response to your prayer.

5

Individual Lament

"When the Individual Hurts"; Psalm 13 as an Example and Practice

The Personal Prayer

WE HAVE BEEN IMPRESSED with the fact that Israel approached God very boldly expressing its desires and needs. We shall find that this intensifies with the individual complaint. This should not be surprising. For here, the I/Thou relationship is strongest. In this social reality, the individual is one-on-one with God. There is no audience, making this a private conversation. The individual may express his or her feelings in a way that may make us uncomfortable, especially in discussions with others. Years ago, I saw a cartoon in a church bulletin that illustrates how we should approach God in lament—humbly and respectively, but directly. In the cartoon, a little girl is saying her bedtime prayers. Kneeling at her bedside, she says, "And now I'd like to tell you about some of the things I'm *not* thankful for." In her most private, one-on-one with God she expressed feelings that one may not think of expressing publicly. Given our negative views regarding complaints to God, many individuals may similarly feel uncomfortable expressing such thoughts to him. We must strive to improve this area of our prayer lives.

To study and observe the major characteristics of individual prayer we should be familiar with the major elements of an individual lament psalm. These include the following, though not every one of these occur in every psalm; nor are they always in this order:

> *Address*—Establishes contact; opening a door; a direct call, for example, "O God!"
>
> *Cry for hearing*—"Hear my cry/prayer/plea."
>
> *Plaint*—Tells God what it is like to be in this situation, asks, "Why?!"
>
> State of the petitioner
>
> Conduct of the enemy
>
> Action or inaction of God
>
> *Petition*—Phrased very generally
>
> For the petitioner
>
> Against the enemy
>
> *Motivation clauses*—Influences God for a favorable response
>
> *Vow*—If God will do this, the plaintiff will do that
>
> *Certainty of hearing*—Expression of confidence (Prayer was heard?)
>
> *Anticipatory praise*—Promises to praise when request granted
>
> *Confession of sin and imprecation*

Psalm 13 as an Example[1]

Opening and Complaint:

> [1] How long, O LORD? Will you forget me forever?
> How long will you hide your face from me?
> [2] How long must I bear pain in my soul,
> and have sorrow in my heart all day long?
> How long shall my enemy be exalted over me?

Plaint/Petitions:

> [3] Consider and answer me, O LORD my God!
> Give light to my eyes, or I will sleep the sleep of death,
> [4] and my enemy will say, "I have prevailed";
> my foes will rejoice because I am shaken.

1. Westermann, *Psalms* 55–59.

Motivational Clauses
> 5 But I trusted in your steadfast love;
>> my heart shall rejoice in your salvation.

Certainty of Hearing/Praise
> 6 I will sing to the LORD,
>> because he has dealt bountifully with me. (NRSV)

The opening and complaint (vv. 1–2) are comprised of the repeated question "How long?" It implies an interruption in the status quo, a dissatisfaction, and impatience. This opening quickly moves into the complaint proper, each introduced by the question "How long?" (1) "How long . . . Will you forget me forever?" (v. 1a). (2) "How long will you hide your face from me?" (1b). (3) "How long must I bear pain in my soul and have sorrow in my heart all day?" (v. 2b). (4) "How long shall my enemy be exalted over me?" (v. 2c). The opening and complaint involve accusations toward God. These are very human and natural questions for a sufferer to ask. Clearly these questions divide into those relating to God, self, and the enemy. They indicate genuineness in this relationship with God, where the lamenter directly and boldly expresses his views and feelings.

The opening/complaint (vv. 1–2) connects directly with the plaint/petition (vv. 3–4) in which the supplicant in the petition asks explicitly that God *fix* the problem. The following table illustrates this relationship.

Opening/Complaint	vs.	Petition
"How long . . . will you forget me forever" (v. 1a) and "How long will you hide your face from me" (1b)	vs.	"Consider and answer me" (3a)
"How long must I bear pain in my soul" (2a)	vs.	"light up my eyes, or I sleep the sleep of death" (3b)
"How long shall my enemy be exalted over me?" (2b)	vs.	"lest my enemy say, 'I have prevailed over'; my foes will rejoice because I am shaken" (4b).

The supplicant boldly and specifically petitions God to fix the situation, to stop the suffering and prevent his possible death. The foundational assumption to these petitions is the belief that the psalmist's petitions regarding his suffering affected God in some way. Further, they demonstrate that human beings cannot always stand uniformly near to God, that God may be remote, and that the supplicant desires to reestablish a closer relationship to God. This would occur if God granted his petitions.

The motivational clauses and certainty of hearing/praise (vv. 5–6), "But I trusted in your steadfast love" and "shall rejoice in your salvation," indicate the supplicant is bargaining with God. In this bargain, he attempts to obligate God to grant his requests. Specifically, he describes to God his condition in the complaints and states what he wants God to do in the petitions. These conclude with the promise to "rejoice in your salvation" (5b) and "sing to the LORD because he has dealt bountifully with me" (6a), which might be described as the certainty of hearing. Therefore, the bargain is straightforward and based on the background assumption stated simply as, "I will tell God that I trusted him in the past and will praise him in the future; therefore, he should answer my prayer." Such bargaining with God is very unfamiliar to many Christians and, as we have noted, often makes them feel uncomfortable. This, however, is the nature of the psalmist's motivational clause. It is respectful, but direct and honest. This individual, like Hannah, possessed a social reality and piety that places responsibilities on the supplicant and God, in which the supplicant obligated himself to do certain things and expects reciprocity from God.

Practice Improving Your Prayer Life

Discuss one or any of Psalms 3–7, 10–14, 16–17, 22–23, 25–28, 35–36, 38–39, 41–43, 51–59, 61–64, 69, 71, 73, 86, 88, 102, 109, and 130 regarding the following questions.

Opening

1. Can you think of an occasion when you asked the above, or a similar question?

2. How would you describe it? What were your inmost thoughts?

Reflection

1. What was the major threat to the individual in this particular psalm?

2. What did the individual particularly ask for in this psalm?

3. Did the individual accuse God, or hold God responsible in any way?

4. Did the individual bring any pressures on God, or bargain with God in any way, to "force" God to deal with the situation?

5. How did the individual expect God to change the situation?

6. Did the person reflect with himself (talk to himself) about anything?

Visualization

1. Can this psalm, or any part of it, function as a model for any concerns we may privately express to God?

2. How does this psalm differ from any of your private prayers to God in times of crisis?

3. Can you think of a time when you had similar feelings toward God about some problem?

4. Are such feelings acceptable to us, to God?

Action

1. Pray explicitly, boldly, and faithfully each day about a problem with which you are dealing. Express exactly how you feel about it to God, knowing that because of Christ he understands. Look to see how God answered your prayers.

2. Keep a diary of your prayer life this week, or write down the prayers you pray. At the end of the week read over your diary or prayers. List things: (a) you would ask for differently; (b) you would not ask for at all; (c) for which God deserves praise.

3. This week, read and reflect on piety in terms of lament and its relationship to praise (Phil 4:7–8) and attempt to express yourself boldly in your prayers, as the Hebrews writer (4:15–16) admonished.

6

Communal Lament

"When the Community Hurts"; Psalm 44 as an Example and Practice

Psalms: 44, 60, 74, 79, 80, 83, and 89

Communal Prayer

WHEN A TRAGEDY STRIKES the community, two levels of suffering occur: the individual and the community. The community will focus on the problems affecting the community as a whole. Most individuals will focus on their immediate problems before that of the community. However, the nature of some people's jobs demand they focus on the community's problems before they focus on theirs. When hurricanes, floods, and other disasters come, individuals in the community have their lives turned upside down due the tragedy. We witness the loss of life and the destruction of homes. Individuals must focus first on these, and then look to the community at large. However, first responders must be out helping these individuals rather than dealing with their own personal issues. For example, when I see a video of a hurricane that has destroyed an entire city, but I see police and firefighters working the scenes of the disaster, I wonder, "Who is taking care of their property?" I imagine, the answer is, "No one." Perhaps I would not have such thoughts had I not witnessed my wife drive through town when tornado warnings were out, because she said, "It is time for me to go to the hospital to work, and staffing says that some cannot report for work." All of this indicates that communal suffering takes on broader dimensions. Individuals suffer, the community suffers, and through it all, some suffer more than others because they honor their responsibility to the community first before themselves. Communal laments occur in this context.

Communal prayer, unlike individual prayer, involves the whole community. The working assumption is that communities pray communal prayers more diplomatically than individuals pray personal prayers. Even so, the maxim "there is strength in numbers" means that the community, unified because of the tragedy, will do heroic things to deal with its issues. Like the individual lament psalms, the communal lament psalms indicate a social reality and piety much different from ours. Because Israel was very comfortable with communal lament, they provide a background for improving our social reality problems exhibited in our different worship styles. To illustrate, one Christian says, "I prefer old songs; they describe our responsibility to God for his care and teaching." Another says, "I prefer new songs; they emphasize our spirituality and relationship with God." Both reflect not only different social realities and pieties from each other, but different social realities and pieties from the psalms. For example, we raised the question in lesson 4, whether any of us have ever attended a prayer service or prayer meeting. As noted there, the only one I ever attended was the one organized by the elders of a congregation where I presented this material. In that case, the church met for the single purpose of praying about issues that were of specific concern. Experiencing one of these demonstrates to the participants their combined strength, unifies, edifies, and builds their faith as they share and pray to God about these concerns. The organization of such meetings may vary according to what is optimal for the group. What do you think would happen should the leaders of your church organize similar, regular prayer meetings?

Psalm 44, an Example of Communal Lament Psalms

1 We have heard with our ears, O God,
   our ancestors have told us,
what deeds you performed in their days,
   in the days of old:
2 you with your own hand drove out the nations,
   but them you planted; you afflicted the peoples,
   but them you set free;
3 for not by their own sword did they win the land,
   nor did their own arm give them victory;
but your right hand, and your arm,
   and the light of your countenance,
   for you delighted in them.
4 You are my King and my God;
   you command victories for Jacob.
5 Through you we push down our foes;
   through your name we tread down our assailants.
6 For not in my bow do I trust,
   nor can my sword save me.
7 But you have saved us from our foes,
   and have put to confusion those who hate us.
8 In God we have boasted continually,
   and we will give thanks to your name forever. Selah
9 Yet you have rejected us and abased us,
   and have not gone out with our armies.
10 You made us turn back from the foe,
   and our enemies have gotten spoil.
11 You have made us like sheep for slaughter,
   and have scattered us among the nations.
12 You have sold your people for a trifle,
   demanding no high price for them.
13 You have made us the taunt of our neighbors,
   the derision and scorn of those around us.
14 You have made us a byword among the nations,
   a laughingstock among the peoples.
15 All day long my disgrace is before me,
   and shame has covered my face
16 at the words of the taunters and revilers,
   at the sight of the enemy and the avenger.

17 All this has come upon us,
  yet we have not forgotten you,
  or been false to your covenant.
18 Our heart has not turned back,
  nor have our steps departed from your way,
19 yet you have broken us in the haunt of jackals,
  and covered us with deep darkness.
20 If we had forgotten the name of our God,
  or spread out our hands to a strange god,
21 would not God discover this?
  For he knows the secrets of the heart.
22 Because of you we are being killed all day long,
  and accounted as sheep for the slaughter.
23 Rouse yourself! Why do you sleep,
  O Lord?
  Awake, do not cast us off forever!
24 Why do you hide your face?
  Why do you forget our affliction and oppression?
25 For we sink down to the dust;
  our bodies cling to the ground.
26 Rise up, come to our help.
  Redeem us for the sake of your steadfast love. (NRSV)

God's Past Conduct, 1–8

These verses remind God of the great things he has done for his people in the past. The conquest of the land was due to God's grace. Israel has been righteous in repeating the story from generation to generation. Interspersed throughout the psalm are individual statements (solos?) which attempt to emphasize and strengthen this relationship (God's blessings and the faithfulness of the community; vv. 4, 6), which demand that Israel will boast and praise God forever (v. 8).

God's Present Conduct, 9–16

God's recent conduct stands in stark contrast to his past. Now God has rejected them (v. 9) as the detailed list of God's deeds against them demonstrates. (1) God has turned them over to the enemy (vv. 10–11). (2) God has sold the people for nothing (12). (3) God has made the community a disgrace before its neighbors (vv. 13–14). (4) The pronouns change from "we/us" (first-person plural) to "my/me" (first-person singular), perhaps indicating a solo inserted into the song in order to describe how the various individuals making up the nation are shamed (15–16).

The Reason Sought for God's Actions, vv. 17–22

These verses seek to establish a reason for God's actions. Yet there is no apparent reason for his anger (vv. 17–19). The community has not forgotten his name (v. 20), nor does that idea make sense to them, for had that occurred, God would have known (v. 21). They draw the erroneous conclusion that God does such things for his sake, and that is the only reason. Therefore, the reason is unfathomable (v. 22). Interestingly, Paul quotes v. 22 and offers an emphatic "no" to this conclusion in Rom 8:31–39.

> What then are we to say about these things? If God is for us, who is against us? He who did not withhold his own Son, but gave him up for all of us, will he not with him also give us everything else? Who will bring any charge against God's elect? It is God who justifies. Who is to condemn? It is Christ Jesus, who died, yes, who was raised, who is at the right hand of God, who indeed intercedes for us. Who will separate us from the love of Christ? Will hardship, or distress, or persecution, or famine, or nakedness, or peril, or sword? As it is written, "For your sake we are being killed all day long; we are accounted as sheep to be slaughtered." No, in all these things we are more than conquerors through him who loved us. For I am convinced that neither death, nor life, nor angels, nor rulers, nor things present, nor things to

come, nor powers, nor height, nor depth, nor anything else in all creation, will be able to separate us from the love of God in Christ Jesus our Lord. (NRSV)

Clearly, Paul is correcting Israel's incorrect piety with which Christians also struggle.

They Petition God to Get Busy and Correct the Situation, 23–26

Throughout, the psalm boasts of the good old days when the community was closer to God and compares it with the sad condition of the present. These are very human and natural statements for the sufferer(s) to make. The statements of this communal lament, as with those of the individual lament, divide into questions about God, self, and the enemy. They indicate genuineness regarding their relationship to God, which produces a structure designed to arouse God to change the present situation. Nowhere do these supplicants confess guilt or even hint at acknowledging wrong. The implication is that God has changed the relationship between himself and the community. The community is sure it does not know why the relationship has changed. The community also knows it has done nothing to bring this change. All the community wants is the relationship restored. Like the individual complaints, they voice complaints that describe their condition, even blaming God for their problems (vv. 9–14), finally concluding that their problems arise due to the inscrutable will of God, which itself is an accusation against God—"Because of you we are being killed all day long and counted as sheep for the slaughter" (v. 22). As a counterbalance to all of this they only offer the petition, "Rouse yourself! Why do you sleep O Lord? Awake, do not cast us off forever" (v. 23). All these feisty, bold statements demonstrate an attempt to pressure God to change his mind.

Practice Improving Your Prayer Life

Discuss one or any of Psalms 60, 74, 79, 80, 83, and 89 about the following questions.

Opening

1. Can you think of an occasion when a community (church, family, etc.) responded to a tragedy with a prayer meeting?

2. If so, how would you describe it? If not, why do you think we do not meet in prayer meetings at such times?

Reflection

1. What was the major threat to the community in this psalm?

2. What did they particularly ask for in this psalm?

3. Did they accuse God, or hold him responsible in any way?

4. Did they bring any pressures on God, or bargain with him in any way, to "force" him to deal with the situation?

5. How did they expect God to change the situation?

Visualization

1. How does this particular psalm differ from our public prayers to God in times of crisis?

2. Can we use this psalm, or any part of it, as a model for any concerns we may publicly express to God?

3. Can you think of a time when your "community" (family or church) possessed similar feelings toward God about some problem?

4. Are such feelings acceptable to us, to God?

Action

1. Hold a second prayer meeting in which you try to express thoughts like those in this psalm.

2. Specifically, meet this week with close friends, or family, and have a prayer meeting about something that is of great concern to that group.

3. Attempt to express yourself in a way like the psalmist. Remember that because of Christ we can boldly approach God.

4. Compare the results of this prayer meeting with the one you held after studying lesson 5.

5. Read and reflect on Phil 4:7–8 and Heb 4:16 as you express yourself to God this week.

7

Proper Social Reality, Piety, and Lament Illustrate . . .

Our Social Reality and Piety Exemplified in Our Prayer Life Relate More to Calvin than the Psalms

WE OBSERVED GENERALLY IN lesson 3 several impressive things. (1) The psalmists' approach to God represented a very bold social reality and piety. (2) This social reality and piety were quite different from that portrayed by either John Calvin or the church today. (3) Because of Calvin's influence, many in the church have failed to venture into the areas of complaint and doubt. Additionally, part of this problem may be due to a Western rather than an Eastern mindset. Our social reality and piety have difficulty reconciling an omniscient, omnipresent, omnipotent, God who: (1) allows our prayers to change his mind; (2) does not act until we have prayed; (3) and often seems far away. Our social reality and piety have trouble looking for God's answers to our prayers when we often look upon such as a coincidence. In short, many perceive prayer—a conversation with God—as one-way rather than two-way communication. An understanding of prayer as *dialogue*, which characterizes both the supplicant and God's character, goes a long way toward helping to clarify certain issues.

How Does Prayer Depict Both the Supplicant's and God's Characters?

Jesus observed, "The good person out of the good treasure of the heart produces good, and the evil person out of evil treasure produces evil; for it is out of the abundance of the heart that the mouth speaks" (Luke 6:45 NRSV). So, when people pray, what they say to God presents pictures of their motives, attitudes, and morality. Similarly, their descriptions of God reveal an understanding of how God may or may not respond to their prayers.[1]

The recorded prayers of Moses, Samuel, Solomon, Elijah, and Hezekiah confirm their status.[2] Their prayers yield images of excellent supplicants. For example, the prayers of Moses, Samuel, and Jeremiah contain terms that portray them as excellent intercessors.[3] This fact begs the question, "Why is there no intercession in the Psalter?" Would one possible answer be, "The individuals who wrote the psalms were not of sufficient status to intercede for others"? Another possible answer may be, "The social reality and piety of the Psalter seem to reflect that each individual should do his or her own praying." Interestingly, our piety seems to focus more on intercession than prayers for self or other concerns. Note the next time you hear announcements regarding needed prayer in the congregation. Nearly all of them involve intercession—praying for someone in the congregation. When issues other than intercession are mentioned they are announced in general terms. Often, this is announced something like, "We need to pray for *so-and-so*," rather than, "Please pray for the following *issues* of concern to us. We are following Jacob's and Hannah's example and asking each member to consider what bargain they would be willing to offer God for him to grant our requests." How do these facts mesh with the commands of Paul, and others who commanded and requested intercession in the New Testament? Could the command for us to

---

1. Balentine, *Prayer*, 48–64.

2. Balentine, *Prayer*, 50–64.

3. Balentine, *Prayer*, 51.

intercede for others overshadow the Hebrews writer's admonition to pray boldly?

How do our prayers characterize us? The prayers of Jacob and Jonah produce caricatures of them. When we compare Jacob's prayer in Gen 32:9–12 to his actions we see his prayer painted a picture of him as humble and obedient while his life exhibited a piety that lived up to his name as a grasper, heel catcher, or one who is faithless. Compare Jonah's actions with his prayers. After he fled "the presence of the LORD" (1:3b NRSV) and the fish, Jonah repented and stated, "But I with the voice of thanksgiving will sacrifice to you; what I have vowed I will pay. Deliverance belongs to the LORD!" (NRSV). Yet, when God spared Nineveh, Jonah was exceedingly unhappy and prayed that he might die, "O LORD! Is not this what I said while I was still in my own country? That is why I fled to Tarshish at the beginning; for I knew that you are a gracious God and merciful, slow to anger, and abounding in steadfast love, and ready to relent from punishing. And now, O LORD, please take my life from me, for it is better for me to die than to live" (4:2, see also 8b and 9b NRSV). Does he demonstrate that an individual may pray the right thing, but then not follow through?[4] Contrastingly, in the Psalter we have no such narrative that furnishes actions to compare with the prayers prayed. Even so, the piety revealed there seems honest in the communication of understanding, point of view, and feelings, whether these were true.

As we have already noticed, Solomon's prayer in 1 Kgs 8:22–53 serves to confirm the temple as a place of prayer for Israel.[5] Further, the very existence of the Psalter testifies of its use somehow in worship, at the temple, and confirms, or hallows, in a special way that edifice. Similarly, when we meet in worship to sing songs and pray to God, those actions hallow that otherwise unholy edifice. While both the Old and New Testaments illustrate that people can pray anywhere, are there places more hallowed than others that are conducive to better prayers? Compare Acts 16:13, for example, where "on the Sabbath day" (NRSV) Paul and his company went

4. Balentine, *Prayer*, 64–80.
5. Balentine, *Prayer*, 80–88.

to the river where they "supposed there was a place of prayer" (NRSV). What of a private space as in Matt 6:5–6, where only the supplicant and God attend? How does praying in a specific place hallow that space?

Prayers also characterize God. Balentine describes how prayers for *divine intervention*, such as Hezekiah's (2 Kgs 19:15–19), Asa's and Jehoshaphat's (2 Chr 14:11; 20:1–5), and David's prayer (1 Chr 29:10–19) each exalt the sovereignty of God, while penitent prayers such as Ezra's, Nehemiah's, and Daniel's (Ezra 9:6–15; Neh 1:5–11; 9:6–37; and Dan 9:4–19), point to a compassionate God.[6] These observations drive us to certain challenging concepts. First, do people of status have greater responsibility for intercessory prayer than those without status? I am sure all of us can think of some devout individual who seems to be on a different plane in their prayer life. What characteristics do these people have that others do not possess? How may we legitimately appropriate the talents exemplified by these prayer warriors?

Second, as with Jacob, does what people sometimes pray not align with who they are? My grandfather told the story of a man with whom he worked who cursed nearly every breath. Yet the man went to worship every Sunday and would not miss a service. One day he told my grandfather that the worship leaders selected him to lead public prayer. My grandfather, unbelieving, asked if he did. The man replied with a profanity saying, "I prayed a _____ good prayer!" Not believing this because the man was so profane, my grandfather went to the next worship service where the man attended. That Sunday the man was passing around the collection. When he came to the pew upon which my grandfather sat, he winked at him! Such a sad case of an individual not taking seriously the most holy nature of worship shocks us. While we condemn such hypocritical behavior, we should each ask ourselves, "Do we often pray prayers that illustrate, 'What we pray is not what we are'?" How consistent is our manner of life with our prayer life? There are going to be inconsistencies, but do we work at bringing our piety and

6. Balentine, *Prayer*, 89–117.

social reality in our prayer life into congruence, or do we continue in a contradictory, unknown, but hypocritical manner?

We must remember that even in all these situations, God is the only one to whom one can turn in prayer and he is a compassionate God, ready to listen and respond. Here is where the crisis in piety and social reality of both the Psalter and our lives exist. Prayers for divine justice, as illustrated by the book of Job, and lament prayers of the Old Testament, including the Psalter, all illustrate that our assumptions regarding God and the real world sometimes do not seem to work.

Social Reality, Piety, Lament, and Their Relationship to Theodicy[7]

"Theodicy" asks the question "Why is there suffering if there is an all-wise and powerful God?" Balentine argues that questions centered in theodicy, if not sufficiently explained, will "destroy the sense of order necessary for the maintenance of society."[8] Obviously, such would also include the more serious issue of its destruction of one's faith in God. We often attempt to explain theodicy events by (a) ignoring them or (b) saying we should not question an all-powerful, all-knowing God.

Laments that arise because of theodicy possess several characteristics, not all of which occur in each prayer. As we have seen, some do admit sinfulness as the reason for the trouble, but this is not the norm, while others seem to emphasize that suffering is in some sense the calling of God's chosen, in which God seems to hide in order to heal and save (Isa 45:15; 53:5).[9]

Other laments admit that one might anticipate suffering, even expect it, because God is God (cf. Job). Such laments indicate that faith has both a place and a legitimate practice for questioning sufferers. Since God never withdraws his promised presence, the

---

7. Balentine, *Prayer*, 139–45.

8. Balentine, *Prayer*, 140.

9. Balentine, *Prayer*, 192.

supplicant may expect God always to hear. Other laments arise out of a sense of powerlessness in which the plaintiff, who is an unequal partner with God, demands that God listen. Other laments attempt to reconcile the existence of evil with the sovereignty of God. Still other laments recognize that they "appeal *to* God *against* God."[10] Therefore, lament becomes the only vehicle open to the supplicants to address issues of theodicy because they seek to explain the unexplainable through negotiations to achieve specific goals.[11]

Balentine argues this understanding of lament has both a positive and a negative side. Positively, the practice of lament presupposes that two parties, though unequal, must be involved in the decision-making process. The greater party takes the lesser party seriously, opening the way for the lesser party to question the power of the greater party. In short, God is available for the petitioner's requests and makes reviewable decisions that may lead to God changing his mind. Negatively, the elimination of lament would sacrifice the dialog between supplicant and God, creating only monologue where God is the only speaker or actor of consequence in a way like that of Calvin. In turn, such monologue promotes either passive silence on behalf of the human partner or pious, but often hollow, words of praise or thanksgiving.[12] "Such a relationship cannot survive the traumas of life, where hurt and pain will not permit a simple 'Yes' or a manufactured 'Hallelujah.'"[13] Denial of suffering follows, which encourages further silence on the part of the supplicant, reinforces the hurt of the hurting, and ultimately negates hope. In short, lament is the legitimate means by which one approaches God and states his case in the hope and faith that he *may* change the mind of God.

---

10. Balentine, *Prayer*, 195.

11. Balentine, *Prayer*, 142.

12. Balentine, *Prayer*, 196.

13. Balentine, *Prayer*, 196–97.

For Review: Elements of a Psalm of Lament

Address—Establishes contact, opening a door, a direct call, "O God!"

Cry for hearing—"Hear my cry/prayer/plea."

Plaint—Tells God what it is like to be in this situation, asks, "Why?!" Gives state of the petitioner, conduct of the enemy, and action or inaction of God

Petition—Phrased very generally, for the petitioner against the enemy

Motivation clauses—Influences God for a favorable response

Vow—If God will do this, the plaintiff will do that

Certainty of hearing—Expression of confidence (Prayer was heard?)

Anticipatory praise—Promises to praise when request granted

Confession of sin and imprecation

For Further Study and Meditation

Opening

1. How do you think our Western mindset affects our prayers and worship?

2. Specifically, do you have difficulty believing that your prayers matter; that you can change God's mind?

3. Do you perceive prayer as one-way communication or two-way communication? Do you perceive prayer as *monologue* or *dialogue*?

Reflection

1. How may our prayers describe our character?

2. How may our prayers confirm our status as pray-ers? Can you think of people close to you who are "prayers par excellence"?

3. Can you think of events in your own life that seem diametrically opposed to what you pray in your prayers?

Visualization

1. Do you have a "holy place," a "prayer room," which is more "holy," that is, more conducive to prayer than other places? If you have such a place, what characteristics influenced you to choose this place? If you do not have such a place, what characteristics do you believe would aid in designating it "a place of prayer" (Acts 16:14)? How may the contents of your prayers illustrate how you conceive of God?

2. Are you uncomfortable with lament, or has this study to this point encouraged you to begin to explore it in your prayer life?

Action

1. Are you beginning to see that our habit of praising God must possess lament as a balance?

2. Do you see how an imbalance might create a false piety where our praise might be hollow?

3. Create an inventory of the prayers you have recently prayed. Can you determine whether you lamented or praised God the most? Reexamine Phil 4:15–16 and create a prayer plan in which you attempt to create the balance that Paul laid out in those verses.

8

Individual Praise

When the Individual Rejoices;
Psalm 30 as an Example and Practice

Psalms: 8, 30, 32, 41, 92, 116, 118, 138

Questions Needing Answers

THE FACT THAT MANY hymnals have few or no lament songs, but constitute primarily songs of praise, indicates an imbalance in our piety and social reality in both corporate and private worship. In a general way, this indicates we have not asked serious questions regarding the foundations of our praise and worship to God. In short, we have predicated our worship on the assumption that we should not lament to God, but offer praise in every situation. We do this without asking certain fundamental questions.

The fundamental questions we should ask include the following. "What is praise?" "Why do we praise God?" "Does it make God any more powerful, better, or more divine?" "Why do we sing songs of praise in church such as 'Worthy Art Thou'"? These questions, if not properly answered, create the unstated belief that praise is useless, or that it we should praise God because he, as God, demands it. Surely, we can provide better answers than these.

Specifically, how does praising God help us, or God? We might improve our understanding of these issues if we asked similar questions on a personal level. Why do we praise one another? Is such praise the response to a joyous occasion? Is it spontaneous or contrived? How does it benefit the one praised and the one praising? How does praise affect the relationship between "praiser" and "praisee"? Individual praise is very personal, and demonstrated in different ways, while public praise proceeds from a different dynamic, and, consequently has different goals and results.

To study the individual praise psalms and their major characteristics we also need to be familiar with the major elements of an individual praise psalm. These include the following, though not every one of these occur in every psalm; nor are they always in this order:

> *Announcement to praise:* Call to praise
> *Summary statement of God's deed(s):* Overview of God's past
> accomplishments
> *Statement of praise:* Describes how God reversed the suffering
> Ties God's action to the praise
> *Vow to praise:* A promise to praise God due to what God has
> specifically done
> This praise will continue after this confession
> This praise begins a new life of praise
> *Descriptive praise:* As a compliment, though not in every psalm

Psalm 30: An Example of an Individual Praise Psalm

We introduced and explored this psalm generally in lesson 4; here we investigate it again in more detail.

> ¹ I will extol you, O LORD,
>   for you have drawn me up,
> and did not let my foes rejoice over me.
> ² O LORD my God, I cried to you for help,
>   and you have healed me.
> ³ O LORD, you brought up my soul from Sheol,
> restored me to life from among those gone down to the Pit.

4 Sing praises to the LORD, O you his faithful ones,
and give thanks to his holy name.
5 For his anger is but for a moment;
his favor is for a lifetime.
Weeping may linger for the night,
but joy comes with the morning.
6 As for me, I said in my prosperity,
"I shall never be moved."
7 By your favor, O LORD,
you had established me as a strong mountain;
you hid your face;
I was dismayed.
8 To you, O LORD, I cried,
and to the LORD I made supplication:
9 "What profit is there in my death,
if I go down to the Pit?
Will the dust praise you?
Will it tell of your faithfulness?
10 Hear, O LORD, and be gracious to me!
O LORD, be my helper!"
11 You have turned my mourning into dancing;
you have taken off my sackcloth
and clothed me with joy,
12 so that my soul may praise you and not be silent.
O LORD my God, I will give thanks to you forever. (NRSV)

The *announcement to praise*, "I will extol thee, O Lord" (v. 1a), is most significant for what follows. It exalts God because the "deed which he performed in someone's daily life is joyfully confessed in the presence of others by the person who can bear witness to it."[1]

The *summary statement of God's deed(s)* illustrates that the worshiper felt compelled to relate everything God had done for him (vv. 1b–3). God lifted him up and did not let the enemies gloat over him—"for you have drawn me up and have not let my foes rejoice over me" (v. 1b). God did this by answering when the petitioner cried for help—"O LORD my God, I cried to you for help, and you have healed me" (v. 2). God's performance of this deed saved his life—"O LORD, you have brought up my soul from

---

1. Westermann, *Psalms*, 77.

Sheol; you restored me to life from among those who go down to the Pit" (v. 3).

The *statement of praise* (vv. 4–5) commands all saints to praise God, describing how God reversed suffering and stating this is the reason for the praise. The saints should "sing praises to the LORD . . . and give thanks to his holy name" (v. 4) because "his anger is but for a moment," but "his favor is for a lifetime" (v. 5a).

The statement that God *reversed the suffering* (vv. 6–10) begins with a statement of the praiser's past confidence as it relates to God's favor—"As for me, I said in my prosperity, 'I shall never be moved.' By your favor, O LORD, you made my mountain stand strong" (vv. 6–7a). Such confidence in prosperity turned to dismay when God withheld his favor—"you hid your face; I was dismayed" (v. 7b). The result was the praiser cried to God and made his petitions (vv. 8–10), which begin with a cry for mercy—"To you, O LORD, I cried, and to the LORD I made my supplication" (v. 8). To this general cry, the psalmist adds the specific, very bold petition—"What profit is there in my death, if I go down to the Pit? Will the dust praise you? Will it tell of your faithfulness?" (v. 9),[2] requesting that God hear his petition—"Hear, O LORD, and be gracious to me! O LORD, be my helper!" (v. 10)

The praiser ties *God's action to the praise* (vv. 11–12a). God heard—"You have turned my mourning into dancing; you have taken off my sackcloth and clothed me with joy" (v. 11). Because God had answered his prayer, he would praise God—"so that my soul may praise you and not be silent" (12a). This vow to praise will continue, producing a life of praise—"O LORD my God, I will give thanks to you forever!" (v. 12b).

Clearly, this psalm of praise makes a connection with a previous successful lament psalm, demonstrating a balance in this psalmist's prayer life. He lamented to God regarding his health, specifically his belief that he would die. He felt impelled to praise God for answering that previous prayer. This pattern arises in Hannah's prayer of 1 Samuel 1, where she prayed to God for a son,

2. We have already noted in lesson 4 how this petition is very bold, stating in effect, "God, if you do not let me live, I will not be around to praise you."

and when God answered her prayer, she returned in ch. 2 to praise him for the answer. Further, this pattern fits with Paul's command of our epigraph in Phil 4:6–7, which ties together anxiety, prayer, supplication, and petitions with thanksgiving. Therefore, Paul recognized a needed balance between lament and praise.

Practice Improving Your Prayer Life

Discuss one or any of Psalms 32, 41, 92, 116, 118, and 138 regarding the following or other questions.

Opening

1. What is praise? Is it a response to God, for blessings received? Is it spontaneous? Does it require previous reflection before it is offered?

2. Do *we* appreciate praise? Does God appreciate it? How do you and I appreciate praise?

3. Can you think of an occasion in which you really "felt the need" to praise God?

4. How would you describe it?

Reflection

1. Was there a reason for which the individual in this psalm praised God?

2. How did the individual specifically praise God in this psalm?

3. What is the importance of the praise elements mentioned above? Why are they important?

4. Did the individual assume any special relationship between himself and God as foundational to any blessings or praise?

5. Did the individual expect his praise to "help" God in any way?

Visualization

1. Can this psalm, or any part of it, function as a model for any praises we may privately express to God?

2. Can you envision any benefit from "private praise"? What is its significance? That is, what benefit arises when the praiser praises the praisee? How does this affect their relationship?

3. Does God need our praise?

4. Depending on your answer to question 3, why should you praise God?

Action

1. Pray explicitly, boldly, and faithfully, attempting to find new ways of expressing praise and thanksgiving to God about particular prayers you feel he has answered. Look to see how God answered your prayers.

2. Read and reflect on Phil 4:6–7 as you express yourself to God. How does the praise relate to the petitions, supplications, and laments?

9

Communal Praise

When the Community Rejoices; Psalm 124
as an Example of Faith and Practice

Psalms: 29, 33, 65, 100, 103, 104, 111, 113, 117, 134–36, 139, 145–50

Communal Psalms of Narrative Praise

As STATED IN LESSON 6 regarding prayer in general, communal prayers exhibit a diplomacy not observed in individual prayers. The primary difference occurs in terms of their presentation. The individual prayers involve just the individual and God, while the communal prayers involve the congregation. Therefore, there is an element of teaching and edification in the corporate worship that does not exist in the private social realty. Even so, both individual prayers and those in corporate worship share some things, such as tying praise issues to past laments. Yet, because the communal praise psalms' social reality is the public context, their praise statements may not be as specific as that of those found in the individual praise. This difference in content between public and private praise prayers may be something that individuals have never considered. We may observe this although God's people have elevated many individual psalms of praise to the public arena for use.

Further, as we noted in lesson 6 when discussing communal laments, because communal praise involves both the individual and the community, the differing personal pieties of the individuals combine in the corporate worship. This synthesis of differing pieties blends into one communal social reality of praise to God. In short, joyous times reflect two levels of rejoicing: individual and community. These two are related. The joy of everyone resounds throughout the worshiping community—again, signifying strength in numbers and the unity it creates, by creating a blended social reality of praise in which each participant edifies the other, producing a multiplying effect of praise to God.

To study the communal praise psalms and their major characteristics we need to review the structure of praise psalms that we introduced in the last lesson. These include the following, though not every one of these occur in every psalm; nor are they always in this order:

> *Announcement to praise:* A call to praise
> *Summary statement of God's deed(s):* Overview of God's past
> accomplishments
> *Statement of praise:* Describes how God reversed the suffering
> Ties God's action to the praise
> *Vow to praise:* A promise to praise God due to what God has
> specifically done
> This praise will continue after this confession
> This praise begins a new life of praise
> *Descriptive praise:* As a compliment, though not in every psalm

Psalm 124: An Example of a Communal Praise Psalm

> 1 If it had not been the LORD who was on our side—
> let Israel now say—
> 2 if it had not been the LORD who was on our side
> when our enemies attacked us,
> 3 then they would have swallowed us up alive,
> when their anger was kindled against us;
> 4 then the flood would have swept us away,
> the torrent would have gone over us;

5 then over us would have gone the raging waters.
6 Blessed be the LORD,
    who has not given us as prey to their teeth!
7 We have escaped like a bird
    from the snare of the fowlers;
the snare is broken,
    and we have escaped!
8 Our help is in the name of the LORD,
    who made heaven and earth. (NRSV)

The *announcement of praise*, "If it had not been the LORD who was on our side" (vv. 1–2a), sets the tone for all that follows. Israel is to state emphatically, to all who will listen, that this blessing was due to God alone. The praise that follows derives from God's past blessing of being the savior of the nation—"If it had not been the LORD who was on our side" (vv. 1–2).

The *summary statement* of God's deed(s), makes the specific point that God saved the community (vv. 2b–5). God sided with Israel "when . . . enemies attacked" them. He prevented them from being "swallowed up alive, when their anger was kindled" against them. God alone stopped the flood that "would have swept [them] away," a flood described as a "torrent" of "raging waters." The poetry employs flood imagery to describe the significance of their rescue from this enemy.

God *reversed the suffering* (vv. 6–7) by providing the escape, described poetically as a "bird" who escapes the "snare of the fowlers," which ties God's saving act to Israel's praise. Israel must praise God because she feels "free as a bird."

The *vow to praise* is absent in this psalm, but the *descriptive praise* occurs in v. 8, and acknowledges that the "name of the LORD" is their help. The praise of God ties specific historical events, though unnamed, to the saving acts of God with which he blessed his people.

Like the individual praise, this communal praise psalm fits with Paul's command in Phil 4:6–7, which ties together anxiety, "prayer and supplication with thanksgiving." Therefore, to repeat, Paul recognized a needed balance between lament and praise.

Practice Improving Your Prayer Life

Discuss one or any of Psalms 8, 29, 33, 65, 100, 103, 104, 111, 113, 117, 134–36, 139, 145–50 regarding the following or other questions.

Opening

1. What is praise? Is it a response to God, for blessings received? Is it spontaneous? Should we think through what we are doing before we engage in communal praise to God? What are some of the issues we should explore?

2. Do *we* appreciate praise, does God, and how?

3. Can you think of an occasion when your family, or worship group, really "felt the need" to praise God? How would you describe it?

Reflection

1. Was there a reason for which the people in this psalm praised God?

2. How did these people specifically praise God in this psalm?

3. What elements manifest them as praise?

4. Did these individuals assume any special relationship between themselves and God as foundational to any blessings or praise?

5. Did these individuals expect their praise to "help" God in any way?

Visualization

1. Can this psalm, or any part of it, serve as a model for any praises we may publicly express to God?

2. Does God need our public praise? Why should we publicly praise God?

Action

1. Hold a third "prayer meeting." Pray explicitly, boldly, and faithfully, attempting to find new ways of expressing praise and thanksgiving to God with this group about particular prayers you feel he has answered. Look for events in your life that you believe indicate answers to your prayers.

2. Read and reflect on Phil 4:7–8 as you express yourself to God.

10

Social Reality, Piety, Lament/ Praise, and Their Relationship

Questions Needing Answers

SOME OF THE FOLLOWING questions we have already introduced and discussed generally. Here, based on the new insights gained, we want to address them again in more detail. We asked the following questions: (1) "What is praise?" (2) "Why do we praise God?" (3) "Does it make God any more powerful, better, or more divine?" (4) "Why do we sing songs of praise in church, e.g., 'Worthy Art Thou'?" (5) "How then does praising God help us?" The answers to these and similar questions usually give the impression that praise is useless. Since we know that is not the case, the answer must lie somewhere.

Social Reality, Piety, Praise, and Their Relationship

Presently across various religious groups, there exists an inability to articulate the purpose and function of praise specifically. The answers most often stated describe the relationship of praise to lament. Miller observes that the purpose of praise functions in two ways. (1) It is a response "to the experience of God's grace and power to exalt the one who is seen and known to be gracious

and powerful and bear witness to all who hear that God is God";
such praise "points back to the supplications and God's way with
the human creature."[1] (2) Such praise acknowledges and confesses
"who God is and in so doing," renders "honor and glory to the one
who is the object of praise," which "is at the same time gratitude
and thanksgiving" for God's "activity in behalf of individuals and
community," and therefore, "makes sense."[2]

Westermann echoes this general idea employing a structural
diagram. He sees praise as being the other extreme from lament;
in short, there exists a "tension-filled polarity of plea and praise,"[3]
in which Israel's prayers moved from lament to praise. This movement toward praise shifts from *lament* to *petition*, in which the
lamenter requests the removal of the cause of suffering, then to
praise, which announces that God granted his petition. This shift
can also occur in reverse, in which praise moves to lament. These
two polar concepts are not in opposition but interchange. "Praise
can retain its authenticity and naturalness only in polarity with
lamentation."[4] This has great ramifications for our piety as it relates
to our social reality. We should expect life to contain joy and sorrow, trial, and good blessing, good and bad. Note the following:

1. To neglect lamentation (which we do) and neglect praise
   (which we sometimes do) reveals a skewed hollow social reality and piety that is hypocritical.

2. To exalt lamentation (which we do not do) and neglect praise
   (which we sometimes do) is to demonstrate a social reality
   and piety that has "no meaning in and of itself."[5]

3. To neglect lamentation (which we do) and exalt praise (which
   we do) is to exhibit a social reality and piety that lose their

---

1. Miller, "Enthroned," 9.
2. Miller, "Enthroned," 11.
3. Westermann, *Praise and Lament*, 154.
4. Westermann, *Praise and Lament*, 267; see also Balentine, *Prayer*, 201.
5. Westermann, *Praise and* Lament, 266.

naturalness and authenticity, producing "mere stereotyped liturgy,"[6] or habit in worship.

4. To exalt lamentation (which we do not do) and exalt praise (which we do) creates a balance in our social realty and piety.

Brueggemann has argued that praise and lament demand that people be loyal to God and not some other god. Therefore, praise involves allegiance; the one who praises emphasizes this allegiance. If there are others who have that individual's fidelity the praise is false. The reason for this situation is the cause for the praise. If the practice (habit) to praise preempts the reason for praise then praise will not build new relationships but defend those already made. This shift may occur three ways.[7]

1. The habit of praise begins to minimize or eliminate the reason for praise. The "concrete memory and experience" for praise is lost; this results in "no reasons for the praise."[8] The worshiper just does it.

2. The specific reason for praise shifts to the recitation of "generalizations which have a bite of neither affront nor energy."[9] The praise becomes meaningless.

3. There occurs a shift from "the motif of liberation to the motif of creation"[10] resulting in such a focus on the good in the present world that there exists no place for the difficult in which the hurting supplicants may petition and praise God in order that God might transform them.

Specifically, if there is no emotional balance, and praise continually occurs without lament (people remain on a high rather than moving back to the depths), praise becomes false, and worship becomes more of a habit, and is ultimately idolatrous.

6. Westermann, *Praise and Lament*, 154.

7. Brueggemann, *Israel's Praise*, 90–104.

8. Brueggemann, *Israel's Praise*, 103.

9. Brueggemann, *Israel's Praise*, 103.

10. Brueggemann, *Israel's Praise*, 103.

The above situations illustrate ways an out-of-balance piety and social reality skews our private prayer life and worship services today. The Calvinistic view of prayer has resulted many times in empty worship services that are out of step with our true feelings. These thoughts go unexpressed due to feelings of guilt. Little wonder that people who are "happy in Jesus," because they may not understand those of us who have serious problems come across as having a simplified piety and are less compassionate in understanding our struggles. No wonder the emphasis on positive thinking, without acknowledging that there are serious depressing things among some of us, has resulted in a false relationship with God in which the first trials cause people to leave God entirely. The imbalance of praise and lament in both private and public social realities reveal a warped piety in which many of us, while claiming to have a *deep* relationship with God, really have no idea how superficial that relationship is. These statements may seem difficult. Yet we must remember that life consists of much more than happiness or sadness. It consists of both happiness and sadness, and we do not ever arrive at perfection in each. We must participate in both, recognizing that these events are part of our spiritual growth, and that lament and praise play a major part in that growth.

Similarly, our relationship with God is not one that will one day reach perfection. Rather it moves from lows to highs, or oscillates between two extremes. Regardless of which extreme, or somewhere in the middle, this pathos of a life with God is the primary ingredient in all of it. *This* is the thing that interests God—our relationship to him. Neither extreme is good or bad, they merely exist and we relate to God accordingly. I believe this is the import of our epigraph in Phil 4:6–7.

The significance of these in counseling and dealing with emotional problems of individuals should be obvious. Any Christian who has this balance in his life is better qualified to deal with any personal issues that arise, as well as help those who need such help. Churches who have this balance can serve their communities better.

Practice Improving Your Prayer Life

Opening

1. Have you created an inventory of your prayer life? If you did, what would you find? Would you find that you possess a balanced prayer life, having about the same amount of lament as praise? If so, what does that say about your view of praising God? Why do you do it? What would be the result if you found you praised God more than you lamented to him or that you lamented to him more than you praised him? Are you as comfortable with lament as you are praise of God, or do you believe you should not lament to God? What would be the result if you created a balance in your praise and lament to God?

2. Can you articulate what Paul was emphasizing in Phil 4:7–8?

Reflection

1. Why do you think we encourage individuals to praise God, while we often discourage people from lamenting to God?

2. How do praise and lament relate to each other in our prayers?

3. Have you in the past had a relationship that allowed you to both lament and praise God?

4. How is lamenting different from complaining?

5. How does praise relate to lament?

Visualization

1. There are about seventy-five lament psalms. How could we use these as models of lament to God in today's world?

2. How might you use the praise psalms to improve your praise of God in your prayers?

Action

1. In the prayer group you created, discuss these issues and try to explain more clearly the bond that should exist between lament and praise. Specifically, address how you might create a balance of lament and praise in your prayer life.

2. Explore how Phil 4:7–8 might function as a guide to creating a more balanced prayer life.

11

Summary and Conclusions

During This Study We Have Learned
Several Facts about the Psalter

THE PSALTER WAS ISRAEL's hymnal. It is composed of five smaller books: 1–41; 42–72; 73–89; 90–106; 107–50. It is composed of several different types of psalms, of which the two main types are *lament* and *praise*. We have compared the psalmists' piety and social reality to our Christian piety and social reality to determine whether our practices were like or different from those of the different psalmists.

We Explored Prayer, Worship, Piety, Social
Reality, and the I/Thou Relationship

Prayer

We asked several questions. What is prayer? Is it communication? Is it a "conversation" between an individual, or a group of individuals, and God? Is it something we "do" as part of our worship, or devotional life? When we pray, does God really listen? How do we *see* God and ourselves? Should we really state our true feelings to God, even when those feelings are feelings that question our faith? For example, should we ask questions like, "Why God did you let this happen?!" Should we bargain with God and try to influence God to do what we think is best? Under what circumstances is it acceptable to complain or lament to or praise God? What part does God play in our prayers? Does God answer our prayers? When, where, and how? How do we expect him to respond to our prayers?

Concerning Piety, Social Reality, and I/Thou

We defined social reality as "the basic dynamics of prayer, or what happens to us (spiritually and physically) when we are 'in the act' of praying." Piety we defined as "all that pertains to the shared perceptions of, attitudes toward, and responses to the divine; that is, how we see ourselves and our relationship to God."[1] We observe the I/Thou relationship involves both piety and social reality. It includes our perceptions of God and ourselves as we worship him. Specifically, when we come to see ourselves as God sees us, we attempt to strengthen our relationship to him by doing whatever is necessary to ensure a continued mutual relationship with him.

We noted that piety, social reality, and I/Thou of the Psalter are most helpful for us. The Psalter focuses not on the transitional moments of the life cycle (birth, circumcision, transition from adolescence to adulthood, marriage, death, etc.), but on the irregular transitional moments (those tragedies and joys which take us by surprise). The people praying in the Psalter were real people. That means they had the same problems you and I have, and they furnish examples for us in our prayer life (1 Cor 10:1–14). They realized and acknowledged adversity and misfortune in the universe. There is a sense of acceptance versus rejection in their personal life (I/Thou). They assumed that if God could impose such concepts on individuals, the reverse was also true—they could place counter-pressures on God.

We saw that these views generally are in marked contrast to those of Christianity as a whole. Christians often assert something like the following: (1) "Why pray at all if God knows everything?"

---

1. Riemann, *Dissonant Pieties*, 57.

(2) "God's will must be done!" "Not my will but thy will be done!" Based on these observations we asked the question, "Is prayer just an exercise for us to get our feelings and thoughts in line with God's will, or do we really believe that our prayers matter, that we can change God's mind?"

We explored Psalm 30 as an example that stands in contrast to the above observations. We noted that this psalm indicates the psalmists possessed a different perspective. Verse 9 illustrates this when the psalmist, self-importantly, states that if he died he would not be around any longer to praise God. The implication is that God needed him.

This examination produced several observations. (1) The psalms do not take it for granted that human interests and divine interests agree. (2) Rather, there is a keen sense of conflicting interests, which can only be resolved through negotiation. (3) The gulf between the human and the divine is real. (4) The petitioners pray for a change in their welfare. (5) They realize that they often approach a line of rebelliousness. (6) These individuals would probably be amazed that Calvin knew so much about the will of God.

We observed that we pray more like Calvin than the psalmists and that part of this problem may be due to a Western rather than an Eastern mindset. Our social reality and piety create the difficulty for us of reconciling an omniscient, omnipresent, omnipotent God with one who: (1) allows our prayers to change his mind; (2) does not act until we have prayed; (3) and often seems far away.

Our social reality and piety have trouble looking for God's answers to our prayers when we look upon such only as coincidence. We perceive prayer as a conversation with God, but as one-way communication rather than two-way communication. If we developed an understanding of prayer as dialogue, in which we looked to see how, when, and where God answers our prayers, we greatly improve our understanding of these issues.

We specifically examined Psalms 13 and 44 as examples of individual and communal lament, respectively. We also examined, Psalms 30 and 124 as examples of individual and communal praise. In the lessons, we created a series of questions whose repetition in the study of any number of lament and praise psalms would encourage further study of the psalms as an example of how they might improve our prayer lives. We continually referred to our epigraphs to see how these served as goals to which we should strive in the improvement of our prayer lives.

Our Study of Lament Psalms Revealed Several Issues

Ignoring the question "Why is there suffering if there is an all-wise and powerful God?" (theodicy) produces faith issues. (1) Faith in God can weaken or it can die completely. (2) We make this problem worse by (a) ignoring it or (b) saying we should not question an all-powerful, all-knowing God.

We observed that suffering produces laments comprising several characteristics. (1) Some do admit sinfulness as the reason for the trouble, but this is not the norm. (2) Others indicate a belief that suffering is something that is in this life never completely understood. (3) Others admit that we may expect suffering *maybe even* because God is God (cf. Job), perceiving that faith has both a place and a legitimate practice for questioning sufferers, since God never withdraws from those in pain; their practice is prayer to the God who promises always to hear. (4) Others arise out of a sense of powerlessness, in which the plaintiff believes God must hear this unequal partner. (5) Others attempt to reconcile the existence of evil with the sovereignty of God. (6) Others recognize that they must appeal to God against God.

The question "What would be the loss if prayer were not possible or effective and if the concerns of theodicy could not be addressed in prayer?"[2] illustrates the importance of lament in our lives. Lament attempts to explain the unexplainable, in which the plaintiff does not engage in self-surrender, but through dialogue becomes a partner with God.

---

2. Ballentine, *Prayer*, 142.

Lament perceived in this manner has both a positive and a negative side. Positively, the practice of lament engages two parties in the decision-making process. The greater of the two parties takes the lesser, unequal partner, seriously. The lesser, unequal partner may question the greater partner. Specifically, the supplicant may question God, leading to a review of divine decisions. Negatively, the neglect of lament sacrifices the interaction between God and plaintiff—dialogue becomes monologue; God becomes the only speaker/actor. This promotes either passive silence on behalf of the human partner or pious, but often hollow, words of praise or thanksgiving. Such a relationship cannot survive the traumas of life. Denial of suffering occurs, which encourages further silence on the part of the would-be plaintiff, reinforces the hurt of the hurting, and ultimately negates hope. In short, lament is the legitimate means by which one approaches God and states his case in the hope and faith that he *may* change the mind of God.

Our Study of Praise Psalms Revealed Several Issues

We raised several questions not usually asked by worshipers. (1) What is praise? (2) Is it a response to God, for blessings received? (3) Is it spontaneous or calculated? (4) Why do we praise God? (5) Does praise make God any more powerful, better, or more divine? (6) Do we appreciate praise; does God; how? (7) How does our praise of God compare to that of the Psalter?

We noted that, as usually answered, these questions give the impression that praise is useless, so the answer must lie somewhere. We observed that some scholars perceived praise as being in interchange with lament, so that prayers move from praise to lament and back to praise. In short, we should expect in life, with all its vicissitudes, joy and sorrow, trial and good blessing, good and bad.

Yet we often neglect lament or praise while exalting the other, which produces specific problems in our piety. (1) To neglect lamentation (which we do) and neglect praise (which we sometimes do) results in a hollow social reality and piety. (2) To exalt lamentation (which we do *not* do) and neglect praise (which we sometimes do) results in meaningless worship. (3) To neglect lamentation (which we do) and exalt praise (which we do) results in a mere stereotyped liturgy. (4) To exalt lamentation (which we do not do) and exalt praise (which we sometimes do) creates a balance in our social realty and piety.

We observed that we have some specific problems with praise. The one who praises God assumes a relationship with God. If that relationship is false, the praise is false. If the habit of praising God becomes more important than authentically praising God then the relationship will not grow but become stagnant. The habit of praising takes the place of the real praise of God. We praise in such stereotyped language that it masks the real worship of God. Praise may focus too much on the goodness of the present order and thus camouflage the hurt and brokenness, which require that one first petition, then praise, God as transformer. If there is no emotional balance and praise continually occurs without lament, people remain on a high rather than moving back to the depths, with the result that praise becomes false, worship becomes more of a habit, and is ultimately idolatrous.

The above produces problems in worship. The elimination of lament, while at the same time exalting the praiser, has resulted in empty worship services that are out of step with our true feelings, which themselves go unexpressed due to feelings of guilt. Little wonder that people who are "happy in Jesus," though they may not understand those of us who have serious problems, come across as being more false than true. No wonder the emphasis on positive thinking, without recognizing that there are serious depressing things among some of us, has resulted in a false relationship with God in which the first trials cause people to leave God entirely. Our imbalance of praise and lament in both our private and public social realities reveal a warped piety in which many of us, while claiming to have a *deep* relationship with God, really have no idea how superficial that relationship is. Life is more than happiness or sadness, it is both happiness and sadness, and we do not ever arrive at perfection in each. Our relationship with God is not one that will one day reach perfection. Praise and lament are interrelated as Phil 4:6–7 show. Whether it moves up or down (Brueggemann), or oscillates between two extremes (Westermann), neither extreme is good or bad, they merely exist and we relate to God accordingly.

The significance of these in counseling and dealing with emotional problems of individuals should be obvious. Any Christian who has this balance in his life is better qualified to help those who need such help. Churches that have this balance demonstrate a greater impact on their communities.

Questions for Further Study:
In the Context of Our Epigraphs
Consider the Following Questions

1. Do you perceive your prayer and worship life differently now than before you participated in this class? If so, how would you describe it?

2. Do you perceive God differently now than you did before you participated in this class? If so, how would you describe it?

3. Do you feel more comfortable in both praise and lament than before you participated in this class?

4. What were the three most important things you learned in this class about yourself, God, and worship? Rank them from the most important to the least important.

5. What changes would improve this class if you participated in it a second time?

Bibliography

Anderson, A. A. *The Book of Psalms.* New Century Bible. 2 vols. Grand Rapids: Eerdmans, 1972.

Ash, Tony L., and Clyde M. Miller. *Psalms.* Austin, TX: Sweet, 1980.

Balentine, Samuel. *Prayer in the Hebrew Bible: The Drama of Divine-Human Dialogue.* Overtures to Biblical Theology. Minneapolis: Fortress, 1993.

Bauer, Walter, et al. [BDAG]. *Greek-English Lexicon of the New Testament and Other Early Christian Literature.* 3rd ed. Chicago: University of Chicago Press, 2000.

Brueggemann, Walter. "The Formfulness of Grief." *Interpretation* 31 (1977) 263–75.

———. *Israel's Praise: Doxology against Idolatry and Ideology.* Philadelphia: Fortress, 1988.

———. *Praying the Psalms: Engaging Scripture and the Life of the Spirit.* 2nd ed. Eugene, OR: Wipf & Stock, 2007.

———. "Psalms and the Life of Faith: A Suggested Typology of Function." *Journal for the Study of the Old Testament* 17 (1980) 4–5.

Buber, Martin. *I and Thou.* Translated by Walter A. Kaufmann. New York: Scribner, 1970.

Calvin, John. *Institutes of the Christian Religion.* Edited by John T. McNeill. Translated by Ford Lewis Battles. 2 vols. Philadelphia: Westminster, 1960.

Gerstenberger, Erhard. *Der bittende Mensch.* Neukirchen-Vluyn: Neukirchener Verlag, 1980.

Harrison, R. K. *Introduction to the Old Testament.* Grand Rapids: Eerdmans, 1969.

Holladay, William L. *The Psalms through Three Thousand Years: Prayerbook of a Cloud of Witnesses.* Minneapolis: Fortress, 1993.

Johnson, A. R. "The Psalms." In *The Old Testament and Modern Study: A Generation of Discovery and Research,* edited by H. H. Rowley, 162–209. Oxford: Clarendon, 1951.

Leupold, H. C. *Exposition of the Psalms.* Grand Rapids: Baker, 1969.

Longman, Tremper, III, and Raymond B. Dillard. *An Introduction to the Old Testament.* 2nd ed. Grand Rapids: Zondervan, 2006.

Miller, Patrick. "Enthroned on the Praises of Israel: The Praise of God in Old Testament Theology." *Interpretation* 39 (1985) 5–19.

———. *Interpreting the Psalms*. Minneapolis: Fortress, 1986.

Mowinckel, Sigmund. *The Psalms in Israel's Worship*. Translated by D. R. Ap-Thomas. Rev. ed. 2 vols. in 1. Nashville: Abingdon, 1962.

Petersen, David L., and Kent Harold Richards. *Interpreting Hebrew Poetry*. Guides to Biblical Scholarship. Minneapolis: Augsburg Fortress, 1992.

Riemann, Paul A. "Dissonant Pieties: John Calvin and the Prayer Psalms of the Psalter." In *Inspired Speech: Prophecy in the Ancient Near East; Essays in Honour of Herbert B. Huffmon*, edited by Louis Stulman and John Kaltner, 345–400. Journal for the Study of the Old Testament Supplement Series 378. London: T. & T. Clark, 2004.

———. *Dissonant Pieties: John Calvin and the Prayer Psalms of the Psalter*. Eugene, OR: Wipf & Stock, 2014.

Watson, W. G. E. "Hebrew Poetry." In *Text in Context: Essays by Members of the Society for Old Testament Study*, edited by A. D. H. Mays, 252–85. Oxford: Oxford University Press, 2000.

Westermann, Claus. *Praise and Lament in the Psalms*. Atlanta: John Knox, 1981.

———. *The Psalms: Structure, Content, and Message*. Minneapolis: Augsburg, 1980.

Printed in the USA
CPSIA information can be obtained
at www.ICGtesting.com
LVHW021012141223
766502LV00036B/671